THE POCKET I CHING

Richard Wilhelm (1873–1930) lived in China for more than twenty years, coming into contact with some of the major Chinese intellectuals of the early twentieth century. Throughout his life he produced a steady stream of translations from Chinese, among the most notable being his translations of the *I Ching* and the *Tao Te Ching*, which is also published in the Arkana series. He was co-author, with C. G. Jung, of *The Secret of the Golden Flower* (Arkana 1984).

THE POCKET I CHING

**THE RICHARD WILHELM TRANSLATION
RENDERED INTO ENGLISH BY CARY F. BAYNES**

EDITED AND SIMPLIFIED BY W. S. BOARDMAN

ARKANA
PENGUIN BOOKS

ARKANA

Published by the Penguin Group
Penguin Books Ltd, 80 Strand, London WC2R 0RL, England
Penguin Putnam Inc., 375 Hudson Street, New York, New York 10014, USA
Penguin Books Australia Ltd, 250 Camberwell Road, Camberwell, Victoria 3124, Australia
Penguin Books Canada Ltd, 10 Alcorn Avenue, Toronto, Ontario, Canada M4V 3B2
Penguin Books India (P) Ltd, 11 Community Centre, Panchsheel Park, New Delhi – 110 017, India
Penguin Books (NZ) Ltd, Cnr Rosedale and Airborne Roads, Albany, Auckland, New Zealand
Penguin Books (South Africa) (Pty) Ltd, 24 Sturdee Avenue, Rosebank 2196, South Africa

Penguin Books Ltd, Registered Offices: 80 Strand, London WC2R 0RL, England

www.penguin.com

This edition first published by Routledge and Kegan Paul, 1984
Published by Arkana 1987
8

The Richard Wilhelm translation copyright 1950
by Bollingen Foundation, Inc., New York, NY
Copyright © Bollingen Foundation Inc., NY, 1967
This edition copyright © Routledge and Kegan Paul, 1984
All rights reserved

Printed in England by Clays Ltd, St Ives plc

INTRODUCTION

The *I Ching* (pronounced 'Yee King') or Book of Changes, the greatest of the Chinese classics, has its origins in the dawn of history. Centuries of development resulted in its becoming the foundation of the Taoist and Confucian philosophies of life. It has exerted a living influence on Chinese life for over three thousand years but has only recently become widely known in the West. It is a work of extraordinary insight and wisdom.

This edition of the *I Ching* has been distilled from the acclaimed German translation by Richard Wilhelm, published in 1924, as rendered into English by C. F. Baynes. It presents the ideas of the *I Ching* directly and simply to meet modern needs. It makes no claim to scholarship neither does it seek to emulate such works. Its purpose is to convey the riches and singular force of the *I Ching* in a handy format for general use. The more abstruse imagery of the original has been omitted in the interests of clarity but the spirit and style of the *I Ching* are preserved.

The *I Ching* is one of the first efforts of the human mind to place itself in the changing universe. The central theme of the work is the continuous change and transformation underlying all existence.

The *I Ching* awaits discovery. Its riches are beyond price. It has no need to justify itself. It is a work of great inspiration that inspired Confucius and Lao Tse and which continues to inspire those who can discern its meaning. It reflects and answers all human conditions. It presents no less than a time-tested philosophy of life.

Its brilliance, clarity and brevity put it above all other writings in condensing so much wisdom into so small a space.

My labour of love in preparing this edition has been to distil, sift and clarify the ideas of the *I Ching* to make the thinking more available and more understandable. I have made no attempt to add to it or to enrich it from other sources. I have sought only that it be clarified and simplified, the better to speak for itself.

A MODERN APPROACH TO THE *I CHING*

The *I Ching* is traditionally regarded as a book with divinatory powers. Even in modern times some of its users suggest that recognition of its occult power is essential to appreciate its meaning and its role.

This is hardly an approach that modern man can be expected to adopt. But neither, on the other hand, can he dismiss the work as so much occult hocus-pocus without doing himself the disfavour of ignoring the most concise, yet most comprehensive, manual of practical moral philosophy ever to have been compiled.

How, then, should he approach it?

According to Confucius, one of the greatest sins is prejudice or closed-mindedness. It is a sustained open-mindedness, so cherished by Confucius, that is required before one can come to terms with the *I Ching*. Like any inspired work, it commands our respect – but not a superstitious or gullible faith in its power of divination.

Whilst it is true that many users feel, at some stage, a sense of its 'remarkable powers', I suggest that what they actually perceive is the book's amazing facility for prompting and making one aware of the remarkable powers of one's own psyche.

The *I Ching* works by the power of suggestion. In 'consulting the oracle', the user first needs to fix reasonably clearly, in his or her mind, a problem area. Having done this (and having, perhaps, written it down to clarify it) he should then approach the *I Ching* with an attitude of respect and open-mindedness. To expect a firm Yes or No answer would be wrong. Almost always, what happens is that the serious user begins to look at his problem in a new way. The *I Ching* works by exploiting the capacity of a receptive mind to draw out linkages between concrete situations (provided by the user) and the abstract but, nevertheless, very pragmatic images provided by the text.

The idea of involving chance as a part of the consultation process is repugnant to some people. None the less, it is, in my view, an essential part of the process because it requires one to respond to the unexpected – just as if one were in conversation with a wise man whose words would not be merely an extension of one's own thoughts.

It is not a book designed to be read, as such, but a companion to live with and get to know and experience over a number of years.

As a prompt and guide in the spiritual life of anyone who seeks, whether they are religious or not, the *I Ching* has a unique place.

THE PSYCHOLOGY OF THE *I CHING*

C. G. Jung, the eminent psychologist, said of the *I Ching*, 'This great and singular book does not offer itself with proofs and results; it does not vaunt itself, nor is it easy to approach. Like a part of nature, it waits until it is discovered. It offers neither facts nor power, but for lovers of self-knowledge, of wisdom – if there be such – it seems to be the right book.'

In summary, Jung's thinking, based on his wide and long experience of the

Western psyche, is that the Western mind is so dominated by the rational, intellectual, scientific approach to life that it often fails to come to terms with the intuitive 'events' that just happen, quite irrationally, as a result of the spontaneous exposure of some facet of the unconscious mind (which is common in character to all humanity, East or West).

This awakening of consciousness of the unconscious (often associated with middle age) is generally a time of marked progress towards the ultimate goal of 'individuation'. However, Jung found that the Western mind tends to shut out intuitive prompts because it falls under the domination of the tyrant, intellect: becomes stagnant and inwardly insensitive. On the other hand, some people become neurotic as a result of a personal incapacity to cope with intuitive, irrational events arising from the unconscious.

The enormous value of the *I Ching* is the way in which it uses its images to expose and develop intuitive dimensions whilst instilling in the user (the seeker) the moral fibre, perseverance and steadfastness needed to balance and accommodate the emerging unconscious in a very practical way. It prompts inward-turning and conscious – unconscious inter-relation but always binds them quite deliberately to the real world.

It brings out the force of inner truth.

It does not hold with the idea of Nirvana sought through inactivity. But it equally posits that any understanding of the real, practical world is utterly dependent upon some measure of awareness of the 'invisible world'. The two must be taken together, with recognition of the immutable 'laws of the universe' (or the cyclic law of change) that govern both in nature and in man, for things to make sense.

In essence, the *I Ching* standpoint is that non-practical spirituality and non-spiritual pragmatism are each as unbalanced as the other.

However, it must also be said, to some people its spirit is clear: to others it conveys little or nothing. Only the reader can decide upon its importance for him.

THE *I CHING* AS A BOOK OF WISDOM

The *I Ching* started life as a book of oracles to be consulted by soothsayers and fortune-tellers. However, to have one's fate foretold, whether accurately or not, provides no moral guidance for the individual as to what he should or should not do in various circumstances.

It was reserved for King Wên, who lived about 1150 BC, and his son, the Duke of Chou, to infuse counsels for correct conduct and ethical standards into the *I Ching*. They transformed a book of divination into a book of wisdom. These roots are reflected in the many wise counsels relating to public life, government and leadership.

Confucius (551–479 BC) devoted much of his later life to reflecting upon the *I Ching* and it is his version, as edited and annotated by him, that has come down to our time.

The insights of the *I Ching* help one to discern in the present the seeds of things to come and, thereby, to foresee the future as well as understand the past. In this sense it is a book of the future.

To understand how a tree is contracted into a seed is to understand the future unfolding of the seed into a tree. To know this movement is to know the future.

Throughout the *I Ching* there is a sense of timeliness or consciousness of the spirit of the time. One is counselled to put oneself in harmony with the ultimate, abiding principles of the universe: to move forward in favourable times and to hold back in unfavourable times. Only thus can one secure one's fate.

The *I Ching* expands possibilities, opens options, exposes psychological blind-spots and aids lateral thinking. It requires one to use one's critical faculties (unlike fortune-tellers). It does not force itself upon one but presents its insights always with an implicit 'Does this make sense to you?' It leaves the reader to draw conclusions: to accept or ignore its counsels.

Throughout history many individuals have been inspired by the *I Ching* in the cultivation of wisdom, detachment, insight, self-knowledge and positive thinking. Confucius himself wished that, had he more years, he would devote them to further study of the *I Ching*.

The book is timeless. Given that allowance is made for social differences like the status of women and the development of democracy, its ideas and moral values are no less relevant in the modern world than they were in ancient China.

THE STRUCTURE OF THE *I CHING**

The fundamental building blocks of the *I Ching* are the ancient concepts of Yang and Yin, representing, respectively, the complementary polarity of light and dark, creative and receptive, heaven and earth, strong and weak, firm and yielding, male and female, positive and negative, movement and rest and so on.

As the thinking matured over centuries this basic Yang/Yin polarity was developed into combinations of Yang (———) and Yin (— —).

* For a detailed study of the *I Ching* structure and line relationships the reader is referred to the Wilhelm/Baynes translation (Routledge & Kegan Paul).

Eight trigrams were derived which were conceived as images of all that happens in heaven and earth. These are:

TRIGRAM		*ATTRIBUTES*	*IMAGE*
☰	THE CREATIVE	strong, active	HEAVEN
☷	THE RECEPTIVE	devoted, yielding	EARTH
☳	THE AROUSING	inciting movement	THUNDER
☵	THE ABYSMAL	dangerous	WATER
☶	KEEPING STILL	resting, calm, firm, quiet	MOUNTAIN
☴	THE GENTLE	penetrating, enduring	WIND, WOOD
☲	THE CLINGING	light-giving, clarity	FIRE
☱	THE JOYOUS	joyousness	LAKE

To achieve even greater multiplicity these eight trigrams were taken in pairs to form sixty-four hexagrams or images. These sixty-four hexagrams, representing sixty-four different conditions or states of change, comprise the text of the *I Ching*.

Each hexagram combines two trigrams:
– a lower or inner trigram,
– an upper or outer trigram.

They frequently relate, respectively, to subjective and objective conditions.

Each chapter consists of four parts:

THE CONDITION – a description of the overall situation or idea.

THE JUDGMENT – associated moral guidance developed from the idea.

THE IMAGE – thoughts derived from the hexagram's image, or its attributes, in giving counsel to a wise man.

DEGREES OF CHANGE – six situations within the overall condition. The DEGREES set out six varieties of condition, often as a progressive development through the overall condition.

USING THE *I CHING*

The reader may wish to use the *I Ching* when in need of solace or as a stimulus to explore alternatives in making decisions. For this purpose the list of hexagrams may help him to find an appropriate chapter.

Alternatively, the *I Ching* may be used chapter by chapter as a source of inspiration for regular meditation: as a guide to help in the cultivation of character.

A third way is to adopt a very old approach, stemming from the origins of the *I Ching*, and to refer to it as directed by the tossing of coins. This is a traditional method of 'consulting the oracle'.

To the Western mind such an approach appears magical or superstitious because it lacks reason or logic. However, to the Eastern mind, the lack of causality is unimportant. It is enough for him that his situation and cast of mind are as much a part of that moment in time as the cast of the coins. The element of chance is deliberately invited into the situation: the same element of chance that, in retrospect, seems to have shaped most of our individual destinies.

'Consulting the oracle' on the basis of tossing coins is recommended. The temporary abandonment of our own efforts to control external events (in this case the choosing of which chapter we should read) accords with the overall *I Ching* philosophy which puts its emphasis, first, upon our reaction to given events. Only then may we seek to gain any influence over them.

In this way, by tossing coins, one avoids taking oneself too seriously (a prerequisite of detachment) whilst, at the same time, preparing one's mind for the serious assessment of an unexpected train of thought and its relevance to one's situation. If the results appear relevant, as is often the case, then it is the interaction between the reader and the *I Ching* that has made them so, not the coins.

The principle of auto-suggestion is essential to the *I Ching*. Consulting the same chapter in differing circumstances will prompt differing trains of thought. It is the reader who infuses such appropriateness as he may find to his specific situation – perhaps by the unlocking of just a little of his unconscious mind.

THE COIN METHOD

Three like coins are taken up and cast down together. This is repeated six times. Each throw gives one line, working upwards.

Each throw gives one of four possible results (lines), counting HEADS = 3; TAILS = 2.

$2 + 2 + 2 = 6 =$ MOVING YIN   symbolised by ──×── ═ ▬▬▬▬

$2 + 2 + 3 = 7 =$ YANG   symbolised by ────

$2 + 3 + 3 = 8 =$ YIN   symbolised by ── ──

$3 + 3 + 3 = 9 =$ MOVING YANG symbolised by ──⊖── ═ ▬▬ ▬▬

MOVING YANG (──⊖──) and MOVING YIN (──×──) lines are considered to have within them so much inner tension that they change polarity and become their opposites.

When moving lines occur the reader is referred to two separate hexagrams: first, the hexagram indicated by the six lines (whether they are moving or not) and then, second, to the hexagram that results from converting all the moving lines to their opposites (i.e. MOVING YANG becomes YIN and MOVING YIN becomes YANG). When moving lines occur the reader's attention is also drawn particularly to the DEGREES OF CHANGE in the first hexagram that correspond with the moving lines, counting from the bottom. (Hexagrams are built up from the bottom so the lines are always counted upwards.)

EXAMPLE

Six throws of the coins produce, in order, the results, 8 7 6, 7 9 8. This translates, starting at the bottom line, into the hexagram ☵̵ , Chapter 47, OPPRESSION. Attention is drawn to the 3rd and 5th DEGREES OF CHANGE (the others may be ignored).

Changing the moving lines in the 3rd and 5th place develops this into the hexagram, ☳ , Chapter 32, DURATION.

In this example one is counselled (Chapter 47) first to recognise that the adverse conditions are exceptional, to see one's oppression, exhaustion, as a test of character and cope with the frustration of not being believed by being strong within and sparing of words.

One is especially advised (line 3) to see one's obstructions for what they are and not to rely on things that have no stability.

One must also (line 5) be patient and firm and inwardly composed.

Then (Chapter 32) can develop the inner gentleness and outward adaptability so essential to the unity and durability of character.

THE HEXAGRAMS NUMBERED ACCORDING TO THE TRADITIONAL SEQUENCE

		above	below
1	THE CREATIVE	☰	☰
12	STANDSTILL (STAGNATION)		☷
25	INNOCENCE		☳
6	CONFLICT		☵
33	RETREAT (WITHDRAWAL)		☶
44	ENCOUNTERING (COMING TO MEET)		☴
13	FELLOWSHIP		☲
10	CONDUCT (COMPORTMENT)		☱
11	PEACE (CONTENTMENT)	☷	☰
2	THE RECEPTIVE		☷
24	RETURN (THE TURNING POINT)		☳
7	THE ARMY		☵
15	MODESTY		☶
46	PUSHING UPWARD		☴
36	DARKENING OF THE LIGHT		☲
19	APPROACH (BECOMING GREAT)		☱
34	THE POWER OF THE GREAT	☳	☰
16	ENTHUSIASM		☷
51	THE AROUSING (SHOCK)		☳
40	DELIVERANCE		☵
62	GREAT SMALLNESS		☶
32	DURATION (MARRIAGE)		☴
55	ABUNDANCE (FULLNESS)		☲
54	THE MARRYING MAIDEN (LOVE)		☱
5	WAITING	☵	☰
8	HOLDING TOGETHER (UNION)		☷
3	RESOLVING CHAOS		☳
29	THE ABYSMAL		☵
39	OBSTRUCTION		☶
48	THE WELL		☴
63	ORDER (AFTER COMPLETION)		☲
60	LIMITATION (DUE MEASURE)		☱

		above	below
26	THE TAMING POWER OF THE GREAT	☰ ☶	
23	SPLITTING APART (DISINTEGRATION)		
27	PROVIDING NOURISHMENT		
4	IMMATURITY (YOUTHFUL FOLLY)		
52	KEEPING STILL		
18	REMOVING CORRUPTION (DECAY)		
22	GRACE (ADORNMENT)		
41	DECREASE		
9	THE TAMING POWER OF THE GENTLE	☴ ☶	
20	CONTEMPLATION (VIEW)		
42	INCREASE		
59	DISPERSION (THE DISSOLVING)		
53	DEVELOPMENT (GRADUAL PROGRESS)		
57	THE GENTLE (THE PENETRATING)		
37	THE FAMILY (THE CLAN)		
61	INNER TRUTH		
14	POSSESSION IN GREAT MEASURE	☲ ☶	
35	EASY PROGRESS		
21	BITING THROUGH (JUDGING)		
64	TRANSITION (BEFORE COMPLETION)		
56	THE WANDERER (THE SEEKER)		
50	THE GREAT BOWL (SACRED VESSEL)		
30	THE CLINGING		
38	OPPOSITION		
43	BREAK-THROUGH (RESOLUTENESS)	☱ ☶	
45	GATHERING TOGETHER		
17	FOLLOWING		
47	OPPRESSION (EXHAUSTION)		
31	INFLUENCE (WOOING)		
28	GREAT HEAVINESS		
49	REVOLUTION (FUNDAMENTAL CHANGE)		
58	THE JOYOUS		

THE TEXT

1 The Creative
2 The Receptive
3 Resolving Chaos
4 Immaturity (Youthful Folly)
5 Waiting
6 Conflict
7 The Army
8 Holding Together (Union)
9 The Taming Power of the Gentle
10 Conduct (Comportment)
11 Peace (Contentment)
12 Standstill (Stagnation)
13 Fellowship
14 Possession in Great Measure
15 Modesty
16 Enthusiasm
17 Following
18 Removing Corruption (Decay)
19 Approach (Becoming Great)
20 Contemplation (View)
21 Biting Through (Judging)
22 Grace (Adornment)
23 Splitting Apart (Disintegration)
24 Return (The Turning Point)
25 Innocence
26 The Taming Power of the Great
27 Providing Nourishment
28 Great Heaviness
29 The Abysmal
30 The Clinging
31 Influence (Wooing)
32 Duration (Marriage)
33 Retreat (Withdrawal)
34 The Power of the Great
35 Easy Progress
36 Darkening of the Light
37 The Family (The Clan)
38 Opposition
39 Obstruction
40 Deliverance
41 Decrease
42 Increase
43 Break-through (Resoluteness)
44 Encountering (Coming to Meet)
45 Gathering Together
46 Pushing Upward
47 Oppression (Exhaustion)
48 The Well
49 Revolution (Fundamental Change)
50 The Great Bowl (Sacred Vessel)
51 The Arousing (Shock)
52 Keeping Still
53 Development (Gradual Progress)
54 The Marrying Maiden (Love)
55 Abundance (Fullness)
56 The Wanderer (The Seeker)
57 The Gentle (The Penetrating)
58 The Joyous
59 Dispersion (The Dissolving)
60 Limitation (Due Measure)
61 Inner Truth
62 Great Smallness
63 Order (After Completion)
64 Transition (Before Completion)

1
THE CREATIVE

▬▬▬▬▬ above   THE CREATIVE, HEAVEN

▬▬▬▬▬ below   THE CREATIVE, HEAVEN

THE CONDITION
The hexagram represents the primal power of Yang: light-giving, active, strong, firm, of the spirit; energy unrestricted, durable.

This power is expressed, first, in the universe in the strong creative action of God and, second, in the human world in the creative action of the holy man or sage in awakening and developing men's higher nature.

The Creative is made manifest only through the effects of its activity.

THE JUDGMENT
   Sublime success through perseverance.
   As creative power permeates all heaven:
   By clouds and rain all beings attain form,
   So the great man sees, with great clarity, causes and effects.
   By persevering does he complete things in their due time.

As the creative power brings forth form from the world of ideas, so the great man understands the meaning of the time.

He overcomes the limitations of the transitory. He understands and gives actuality to the way of the universe:

Each end is a new beginning.

Time is the instrument of the Creative. It ceaselessly moves, develops, transforms, shapes and furthers all beings in accord with their true natures; it keeps them in conformity with the Great Harmony.

As the Creative perseveres, so also the great man perseveres: creating order, thence peace, security and union for all.

Here abide the four cardinal virtues of humanity: love, morality, justice and wisdom. Love embraces all. Morality regulates love. Justice furthers true nature in all beings. Wisdom discerns the great laws of change and so can bring about enduring conditions.

THE IMAGE
   As heaven moves with unceasing power,
   So the wise man becomes strong, untiring.

Heaven upon heaven means duration both in and beyond time. As one day follows upon another in unending course, so the Creative never stops nor slackens.

Thus does the sage learn to develop himself so that his influence may endure.

Only by consciously limiting the fields of one's activity can one attain tirelessness.

2

DEGREES OF CHANGE

1. *Creative power that is still hidden.*
   When the time is not ripe, do not act.

In winter the creative power withdraws and has no effect. So too a great man, as yet unrecognised, remains true to himself. He is not swayed by outward success or failure. He bides his time in the calm strength of patience. One must not expend one's powers prematurely, when the time is not yet ripe.

2. *Creative power that stirs in the field.*

In spring the effects of the Creative begin to show. Likewise does the influence of the great man begin to be felt in his chosen field of activity. He is distinguished not by his high rank but by his seriousness of purpose, unqualified reliability and effortless influence.

3. *Creative power that becomes known.*
   But dangers lurk in the rise to fame.

As a great man's fame and influence grow people flock to him. He needs inner power, moral stability, to balance his increased outward activity. Many great men have been ruined by being swept into the course of their following. Ambition destroys integrity. Be prudent and stay blameless.

4. *To weigh and waver. Where is one's way?*

At a great man's moment of transition he must choose. Should he soar to great heights and worldly importance or withdraw into solitude to develop himself? Hero or secluded sage? No general law says which is right. But he must accord with the inner law of his being, be consistent and true to himself to be without blame. He has a free choice. Each man must determine his own fate.

5. *Creative power accords with heaven.*

A great man at work accords with heaven and so his influence spreads everywhere. As water flows to what is wet and fire turns to what is dry so, by inner affinity, what is born of heaven accords with what is above: what is born of earth with what is below. Each follows its own kind. To follow the great man: therein is blessing.

6. *Creative power that goes too far:*
   Arrogance will bring cause to repent.

If one seeks to climb so high that one loses touch with others, one will become isolated. Titanic aspirations, beyond one's powers, always lead to failure. By the law of change, what is too full cannot last.

2

THE RECEPTIVE

≡≡ above   THE RECEPTIVE, EARTH

≡≡ below   THE RECEPTIVE, EARTH

THE CONDITION

THE RECEPTIVE, the primal Yin nature, is the complement, not the opposite, of THE CREATIVE. It does not combat THE CREATIVE but completes it. It is earth as against heaven; nature as against spirit; wife as against husband; son as against father or an official as against his ruler.

THE RECEPTIVE represents one who serves, one who takes second place, one who is yielding, devoted, moderate and correct.

Whilst THE CREATIVE initiates things, THE RECEPTIVE brings them to birth and gives them bodily form.

THE CREATIVE acts in movement and rests in standing still: THE RECEPTIVE acts in opening out and rests in closure.

In opening, THE RECEPTIVE allows divine light to enter and thereby illumines everything: in closure, in resting, it embraces all things as in a vast womb.

THE JUDGMENT

THE RECEPTIVE is strong, yet devoted.
If one tries to lead, one loses oneself.

Following with devotion is the nature of the Receptive. One should not strive to achieve everything of one's own strength but keep receptive to guiding influences.

The Receptive must be led by the Creative. When it seeks to stand equal with the Creative, it becomes evil.

But being yielding and devoted must not exclude strength. Consider the mare, tirelessly roaming the vast expanse of the earth. She is strong and swift as a horse yet gentle and devoted as a cow.

Be likewise: tireless, strong, devoted.

THE IMAGE

As is the earth's nature: strong, devoted,
Thus does a wise man carry the outer world.

The earth is broad and massive, carrying all things, good and evil, without exception. It does not, thereby, forfeit its nature.

Thus does the wise man, with breadth and weight of character, carry the outer world. By inner strength and breadth of view can one endure the world without being swayed by it.

Inner life becomes right by the way of consistent seriousness. Outer life becomes correct through fulfilment of duty.

DEGREES OF CHANGE

1. *When hoarfrost is underfoot*
   Solid ice is not far off. Be vigilant.

Be warned. Do not minimise the beginnings of evil. Left to itself, evil grows as inevitably as ice follows the hoarfrost of autumn. So, take heed of the first signs of decay and check them in time.

2. *Be like nature: true, calm and great;*
   Without design, yet furthering all.

Nature is true, does not err, in creating all beings; calm and still in tolerating all creatures equally. She uses no artifice. This is greatness. So too, one achieves the height of wisdom when all one does is as right and as self-evident as is nature. Thus is one's rightness assured. But doubts induce timid vacillation: they lame the power of decision. Be dutiful, consistent, true.

3. *Seek not works, but bring to completion.*
   Thus can one remain persevering.

If one is free of vanity, one can conceal one's abilities for a time, thus to mature undisturbed. If one enters public life, do so with restraint. A wise man gladly leaves fame to others. Like the earth, he does not seek credit, but work that will bear fruit.

4. *When in danger, strictest reticence.*

Any degree of prominence is dangerous because it leads either to enmity, if one challenges others, or to misunderstanding, if one lacks firmness. Be it in solitude or in the turmoil of the world, be cautious and reserved. By hiding oneself, one is, at least, free of obligations. No blame. No praise.

5. *Genuineness and utmost discretion.*
   Gracefulness comes from within.

Genuineness and refinement should not show directly, but be expressed only indirectly as effects from within. So, be reserved. If one is given prominence, true success lies in utmost discretion. One is never independent. Be ready to yield precedence.

6. *If one tries to rule, one is overthrown.*

If one tries to maintain a position to which one is not entitled; to rule rather than to serve, one draws down upon oneself the anger of the strong. Such struggle injures both sides. This unnatural contest between Yang and Yin principles only arises because the dark principle is presumptuously seeking to take the leadership for itself by entering into rivalry with the light principle.

3
RESOLVING CHAOS

above	THE ABYSMAL, WATER
below	THE AROUSING, THUNDER

THE CONDITION
Thunder and rain fill the air. It is as if heaven and earth encounter each other for the first time. Like a difficult first birth, their meeting is beset with difficulties.

The trigrams' attributes, arousing within and danger without, give the idea of teeming, chaotic profusion.

The motion of the lower trigram, THE AROUSING, is upward: that of the upper trigram, THE ABYSMAL, is downward. As THE ABYSMAL sinks, the upward arousing movement passes to beyond the danger. Thus is the chaos resolved: like a thunderstorm, it brings release from tension and all things breathe freely again.

THE JUDGMENT
Chaos and darkness whilst heaven creates.
In times of difficulty at the beginning,
Persevere. Appoint helpers. Do not rest.
For in this way comes success.

Times of growth are beset with difficulties at their beginnings, arising from the very profusion of all that is struggling to attain form. Everything is in motion. But, in spite of danger, there is the prospect of success.

When it is one's fate to undertake new beginnings, when everything is still unformed, one must hold back. Any premature move may bring disaster.

It is important not to remain alone. One needs able helpers to overcome chaos. One should appoint them but not, thereby, be lulled to rest, or look on passively, or rely wholly on others. One should participate with inspiration and guidance. That is one's work.

As storms bring release in nature, so too, in the world of men, chaotic times precede a period of order.

THE IMAGE
By movement in the midst of danger,
The wise man brings order out of confusion.

Clouds and thunder both have their place: order is already implicit. So too, the wise man arranges and organises the chaotic profusion of new beginnings.

Just as one sorts out silk threads from a tangle to bind them into skeins, so one must be able both to separate and to unite, if one is to find one's place in the infinity of being.

DEGREES OF CHANGE

1. *Hesitation; hindrance. Appoint helpers.*
   Be steadfast. Rule by serving. Success.

If one is hindered at the beginning of an enterprise, do not try to force advance. Pause. Take thought. But let nothing put one off one's course. Persevere. Keep the goal in sight. It is important to seek out helpers. One can find the right people only by avoiding arrogance and meeting one's fellows in a spirit of humility. When an eminent man thus subordinates himself to his inferiors, he wins the hearts and minds of all.

2. *If unexpected relief comes, be cautious.*

When, in times of difficulty, an unexpected relief is offered from a source unrelated to us, we must take care not to commit ourselves to any obligations entailed; otherwise, we impair our freedom of action. If we bide our time, things will become quiet and our hopes will be fulfilled. Pledge yourself with care.

3. *With no guide, a wise man will desist.*

Difficulties must be faced: we cannot dupe fate. But premature effort, without the necessary guidance, will end in failure and disgrace. A wise man can discern the seeds of coming events. He would, therefore, rather renounce a wish than provoke humiliation.

4. *An opportunity. It must be seized.*
   Let neither false pride,
   Nor false reserve, deter one.

When it is our duty to act, we should do so, even though we lack the power. Taking the first step, even though it involves self-abnegation, indicates inner clarity. To accept help in difficulties is no disgrace, if the helpers are right.

5. *When others interpose*
   And distort one's intentions,
   One must be cautious, not forceful.

If one's good intentions are hindered from being understood and taking shape, one must be cautious. Proceed step by step. Success is only possible when general confidence prevails. Do not force advance. One should carry on with faithful, unobtrusive, conscientious work until the cloud lifts.

6. *Despair. Bloody tears flow.*

Resolving chaos is too much for some people. They get stuck and give up the struggle. How sad. They should quickly try to make a clean break and begin a new beginning. In this way can the standstill be overcome.

4

IMMATURITY (YOUTHFUL FOLLY)

≡≡ above KEEPING STILL, MOUNTAIN
≡≡ below THE ABYSMAL, WATER

THE CONDITION

Folly here means inexperience, immaturity, rather than mere stupidity.

A spring rises at the foot of a mountain. It gushes forth not knowing which way it will go: the confusion of inexperienced youth.

The attributes, danger and standstill, suggest stopping on the brink of a dangerous abyss: the perplexity of youth.

But out of the confusion, perplexity and obtuseness of youth comes enlightenment.

THE JUDGMENT

> *It is not I who seek the young fool:*
> *It is the young fool who seeks me.*
> *At first, I inform him with clear answers;*
> *But if he importunes, I tell him nothing.*
> *He must persevere to succeed.*

The text counsels both teacher and pupil. The youth must be conscious of his lack of experience and must seek out the teacher. Without this modesty, this respectful acceptance of the teacher, there is no guarantee that he has the necessary receptivity.

The teacher must wait to be sought out instead of offering himself: this is the correct relationship in education.

A teacher's answers to a pupil should be clear and definite: to resolve doubts and provide a basis for decision.

But if mistrustful or unintelligent questioning is kept up it serves to annoy the teacher. He does well to ignore it in silence.

Youthful folly, inexperience, leads to success only by perseverance that never slackens until all the points are mastered one by one: a thoroughness that skips nothing but fills up all the gaps and so flows onward.

To strengthen what is right in a fool is, indeed, a holy task.

THE IMAGE

> *As a clear mountain spring flowing onward,*
> *So is the wise man: thorough, clear and calm.*

As a spring flows on (avoids stagnation) only by filling all the hollow places in its path, thus does a wise man foster his character: thoroughgoing, he attains the clarity of a mountain spring.

Like the great calmness of a mountain on the edge of an abyss, he achieves calmness in the face of danger.

DEGREES OF CHANGE

1. *To make a fool develop, use discipline.*
   But as self-discipline grows,
   The fetters should be removed.

Youth, careless and playful, must be shown the seriousness of life. He who plays with life never amounts to anything, but taking oneself in hand, brought about by strict discipline, is a good thing. Discipline should not degenerate into mere drill: drill has a crippling effect if continued unduly.

2. *To bear with fools kindly brings favour.*

One needs inner strength rather than external power to bear one's burden of responsibility and tolerate, with kindliness, the shortcomings of human folly. Like a son, required to take charge of the household, one must show chivalrous consideration towards the weaker. It is only inner strength and outer reserve that enable one to take on social responsibilities with success.

3. *Like a foolish girl, one loses oneself.*

Like a foolish girl, throwing herself away, a weak, immature man, struggling to rise, can easily lose his own individuality by slavishly imitating a stronger personality of higher station. Such servility is bad for both youth and teacher. As a girl owes it to herself to wait until she is wooed, so also it is undignified to offer oneself. Nor does any good come of accepting such an offer.

4. *Entangled folly brings humiliation.*

When a youth is hopelessly entangled in empty imaginings and is obstinately preoccupied with unreal fantasies, he should be left to himself for a time and not be spared the humiliation that results. This is frequently the only means of rescue.

5. *Childlike folly brings good fortune.*

An inexperienced person who seeks instruction in a childlike and unassuming way is on the right path. One who is devoid of arrogance, gentle, devoted and ready to listen, who subordinates himself will surely be helped.

6. *Punish folly: but only to restore order.*

When an incorrigible fool must be punished, the penalty should not be imposed in anger. Punishment is never an end in itself, but serves only to restore order, to guard against unjustified excess. That is its objective.

Likewise, the interventions of government should always be merely preventative: solely aimed at restoring peace and security.

5

WAITING

above   THE ABYSMAL, WATER

below   THE CREATIVE, HEAVEN

THE CONDITION

Clouds in the heavens provide nourishment from above: rain to refresh all that grows, to nourish mankind with food and drink.

But the gift of food comes in its own time and, for this, we must wait. We cannot make the rain come. We have to wait for it.

The idea of waiting is suggested by the trigrams' attributes: strength within and danger in front. Strength, in the face of danger, does not plunge ahead but bides its time. It is weakness in the face of danger that grows agitated and has not the patience to wait.

THE JUDGMENT

If you are sincere: light and success.
Be firm, strong, within; thus one avoids
*   the danger of perplexity, bewilderment.*
Resolution equips one to meet one's fate.

Waiting means not advancing, holding back. Waiting does not mean giving up an undertaking: to defer is not to abandon.

Waiting is not mere empty hoping. It has the inner certainty of reaching the goal. Only such certainty gives that light which leads to success. Faced with danger, weakness and impatience can do nothing.

Only a strong man can stand up to his fate. His inner security enables him to endure to the end. His strength shows in uncompromising truthfulness with himself: courage to face reality without illusion or self-deception.

Only when we have the courage to face things exactly as they are can we see the path.

Patient waiting is particularly essential for one who rules. It is only by the steadfastness of continuous influence that a ruler can bring his plans to fruition.

THE IMAGE

When clouds rise up to heaven
The wise man eats and drinks.
He is joyous and of good cheer.

When clouds rise up in the sky it will not be long before rain comes. The wise man accepts and adapts to the situation.

When destiny is at work we should not worry or interfere in things before the time is ripe. We should fortify ourselves with food and drink, gladness and good cheer.

Thus, when fate comes, we are ready.

DEGREES OF CHANGE

1. *When the danger is still far away,*
   Waiting in a tranquil place. No blame.

The danger is not yet close. Conditions are simple, yet there is a feeling of something impending. One must continue to lead a regular life as long as possible and so guard against a premature waste of strength.

One must keep free from error and blame for that would be a source of weakness later on. Remain calm and collected.

2. *The danger appears. Gossip. Keep calm.*

The danger gradually comes closer. Disagreements and general unrest can easily develop in such times and we blame one another. He who stays calm will succeed in the end. Slander will be silenced if we do not gratify it with injured retorts.

3. *Entangled in danger. Be cautious.*

The danger comes closer. The enemy arrives. Instead of gathering strength to overcome the danger, at one try, one has made a premature start and got no further than entanglement. One thus invites one's enemies to take advantage. Only by being cautious, sensible and serious can one keep oneself from injury.

4. *Extreme danger. Get out of the pit.*

The danger is now of the utmost gravity. It is a matter of life and death. One can go neither forward nor backward. One must simply stand fast and let fate take its course. Such composure keeps us from aggravating the trouble. It is the only way out.

5. *Waiting at meat and drink. Good cheer.*

Even in the midst of danger intervals of peace occur. If we possess inner strength we will take advantage of them to fortify ourselves for renewed struggle. We must know how to enjoy the moment without being deflected from the goal.

6. *One falls into the pit. Stay alert.*
   Outside intervention brings rescue.

The danger can no longer be averted. One falls into the pit and must yield to the inevitable. All seems to have been in vain. Precisely in this extremity, events turn. Without a move on one's own part there is outside intervention. But one is unsure. Is this rescue or destruction? Keep alert. Do not withdraw into oneself with a sulky gesture of refusal. Greet the new turn with respect and deference. Even happy turns of fate can appear strange at first.

6
CONFLICT

≡≡ above   THE CREATIVE, HEAVEN

≡≡ below   THE ABYSMAL, WATER

THE CONDITION
In three ways is conflict represented:

* Heaven's nature is to rise upward, water's nature is to flow downward. The trigrams' tendencies are to move away from each other, hence the idea of conflict.

* The trigrams' attributes are danger (inner guile) and strength. Where cunning has force before it, there is conflict.

* In terms of character, inner cunning and fixed outward determination indicate a person who is sure to be quarrelsome.

THE JUDGMENT
You are sincere but are obstructed,
A cautious halt halfway brings favour;
Going through to the end brings disfavour.
Take advice. Seek a just arbiter.
Great undertakings are not favoured.

Conflict develops when one feels in the right but one runs into opposition. If one is not sure of being in the right, opposition leads to craftiness or high-handed encroachment, but not to open conflict.

One entangled in conflict must be so clear-headed and inwardly strong that he is always ready to meet his opponents halfway.

To carry out a conflict to the bitter end, even when one is right, breeds enmity and will surely have evil effects.

An arbiter must be a great, impartial man with the authority to terminate the conflict amicably or assure a just decision.

In times of strife, dangerous enterprises or great undertakings should not be begun because, to succeed, they require the concerted unity of forces.

Conflict must not be allowed to become permanent.

When conflict is within it weakens the power to conquer danger without.

THE IMAGE
Heaven and water go their opposite ways.
A wise man considers his plans' beginnings.

In the image, the causes of conflict are already latent. When opposing tendencies appear, conflict is inevitable.

One avoids this by ensuring that rights and duties are exactly defined, or that, in a group, the spiritual trends of the individuals harmonise. Thus can one remove the cause of conflict in advance.

DEGREES OF CHANGE

1. *One should not perpetuate the affair.*
   Despite gossip, blessing will come.

In the first stages of conflict the best thing to do is to drop the issue. Especially when the adversary is stronger, it is not advisable to push conflict to a decision. It may come to a slight dispute but, in the end, justice will prevail.

2. *If one cannot engage in conflict*
   Then give way. Remain free of guilt.

In a struggle with an enemy of superior strength, retreat is no disgrace. Timely withdrawal prevents bad consequences. To contend from a lowly place with someone above brings self-incurred suffering. A wise and conciliatory attitude benefits the whole community as it then avoids being drawn into the conflict.

3. *Contemplate ancient virtue. Persevere.*
   If you serve a ruler, seek not works.

Whatever one possesses in the strength of one's own nature, induced by contemplating ancient virtue, cannot be lost. But there is danger in a restless, expansive disposition. In serving a superior, conflict will surely arise if one seeks works for the sake of personal prestige. Let it be enough if the work is done. Let the honour go to another.

4. *If one cannot engage in conflict against the weak, one should*
   turn back.
   Changing one's attitude, one finds peace.
   Persevere this way.

If one lacks inner peace because one has a weaker opponent and, despite the prospect of success, one cannot justify this to one's conscience, then one should turn back. To accept one's fate is to find lasting peace.

5. *If one is in the right, seek an arbiter.*
   Then, to contend brings good fortune.

An arbiter must be powerful and just. A dispute may be turned over to him with confidence. If one is in the right, one will attain good fortune.

6. *One has triumphed. One is decorated.*
   But one's happiness does not last.

One has carried a conflict to the bitter end and one has triumphed. But one is attacked again and again and the conflict perpetuated. One will have cause to rue the matter. To attain distinction through conflict is, after all, nothing to command respect. What is won by force is wrested away by force.

7

THE ARMY

≡≡ above THE RECEPTIVE, EARTH
☵ below THE ABYSMAL, WATER

THE CONDITION

The trigrams give the idea of ground water stored up in the earth. In the same way, military strength is stored up in the mass of the people: invisible in times of peace but always ready for use as a source of power.

The trigrams' attributes show the nature of an army: dangerous at the core, within, yet discipline and obedience prevail.

THE JUDGMENT

THE ARMY. It needs steadfast discipline,
Perseverance and a strong man to unite. ‹

An army is a mass that needs organisation to become a fighting force. Without strict discipline nothing can be accomplished.

But this discipline must not be achieved by force. It requires a strong man who can capture the hearts of the people and awaken their enthusiasm.

To develop his abilities he needs the complete confidence of his ruler, who must entrust him with responsibility as long as the war lasts. War is dangerous, like a poisonous drug: it brings destruction and devastation. Therefore, it should not be resorted to rashly but as a last recourse.

The justifying cause of war and clear, intelligible war aims need to be explained to the people by an experienced leader. Without definite aims, to which the people can consciously pledge thenselves, the unity and strength of conviction that lead to victory will not be forthcoming.

The leader must also ensure that the passion of war and the delirium of victory do not give rise to unjustified acts. Justice and perseverance must always prevail.

THE IMAGE

As the earth shelters waters within it;
So does a wise ruler increase his wealth:
By generosity towards his people.

People who live under a mild rule become strong and powerful. To win respect as a military power depends on economic strength. Such power must be cultivated by improving the economic condition of the people and by humane government. In this way is formed an invisible bond between people and state. He who rules this way fosters the people: he finds devotion and wins love.

DEGREES OF CHANGE

1. *An army must set forth in proper order.*
   If the order is not good, misfortune.
At the beginning of a military action order is imperative. A just and valid
cause must exist and the obedience and co-ordination of the troops must be
well-organised. Joyousness is not the proper frame of mind for the onset of
war.

2. *The leader of the army is decorated.*
The second line, strong and uniting, represents the leader in the midst of the
army, in touch with it and sharing good and bad with those he leads. This
alone makes him equal to the heavy demands made upon him. The ruler
recognises this and decorates him, not for personal preferment, but to honour
the whole army. Such is grace from heaven upon one who has the welfare of
all nations at heart.

3. *Too many ride in the wagon. Misfortune.*
When someone other than the chosen leader interferes with the command,
authority is not being exercised by the proper leaders, but has been usurped
by others. This is without merit: it leads to defeat.

4. *The army retreats. No blame.*
When faced by a superior enemy, an orderly retreat is the only correct
procedure because it will save the army from defeat and disintegration. It is by
no means a sign of courage and strength to insist upon engaging in a hopeless
struggle, regardless of the circumstances.

5. *An enemy invades. Let the eldest lead.*
If an enemy encroaches, energetic combat and punishment are well-justified.
But this must not degenerate into a wild melèe, with everyone fending for
himself. Despite the greatest perseverance and bravery, this would lead to
defeat and misfortune. It is a matter of waging war, not of permitting the mob
to slaughter all who fall into their hands. An army must be directed by an
experienced leader: let the younger carry the corpses.

6. *The king rewards merit with position.*
   But small people he does not employ.
The war has ended. Victory is won. The ruler gives estates and positions to
his faithful vassals. But it is important that inferior people should not come to
power. If they have helped, let them be paid off with money; but let them not
be awarded lands or the privileges of power, lest power be abused.

8
HOLDING TOGETHER (UNION)

≡≡ above THE ABYSMAL, WATER
≡≡ below THE RECEPTIVE, EARTH

THE CONDITION

The waters on the surface of the earth flow together wherever they can into rivers and oceans. Hence the idea of union.

Holding together means mutual help.

The five yielding Yin lines of the hexagram hold together because they are united and influenced by a man of strong will in the leading position. He is the centre of union.

Moreover, this strong, guiding personality, in turn, holds together with the others, finding in them the complement of his own nature. He ensures that each member finds his true interest in holding together.

THE JUDGMENT

HOLDING TOGETHER brings blessing.
Do you possess the sublimity, constancy,
And perseverance to be the centre of union?

To become a centre of influence is a grave matter, fraught with great responsibility. It requires greatness of spirit, consistency and strength.

Therefore, let him who would gather others about him, ask himself if he is equal to the undertaking; for anyone attempting the task without a real calling only makes confusion worse than if no union at all had taken place.

If one recognises the need for union, but one does not feel strong enough to function as the centre, it is one's duty to join some other organic fellowship.

Relationships are formed and established in accord with definite inner laws. Common experiences strengthen these ties. When there is a real rallying point, those at first hesitant gradually come in of their own accord. But he who comes too late to share in these basic experiences must suffer if he finds the door locked.

THE IMAGE

As waters over the earth flow together,
So a wise ruler cultivates relationships.

As water flows to unite with water, because all parts of it are subject to the same laws, so too should human society hold together through a community of interests that allows each to feel himself a member of the whole.

A wise leader, in any society, must see to it that every member finds his true interest lies in holding together with it.

DEGREES OF CHANGE

1. *Holding together depends on sincerity.*
   Sincerity is like a full earthen bowl.
   Hold to him in truth and loyalty.

Fundamental sincerity is the only proper basis for relationships. Like a full earthen bowl: the content is everything, the empty form is nothing. Sincerity shows itself not in clever words but through inner strength so great that it has the power, even in a lowly place, to attract good fortune to itself from without.

2. *Inner loyalty. But do not lose yourself.*

If one responds perseveringly, and in the right way, to behests from above that summon one to action, one's relations with others will be intrinsic: one does not lose oneself. But if a man seeks association with others just to gain favours, or if he depends on unworthy external manoeuvres, he throws himself away. A wise man never loses his dignity: he is reserved; never obsequious.

3. *Holding together with the wrong people.*

One is often among people not of one's own sphere. Beware of being drawn into false intimacy through force of habit. Maintain sociability without intimacy. This is the only right attitude, otherwise one would not be free to enter into relationship with people of one's own kind later on.

4. *When one may also show outward loyalty.*

One's relations with the centre of union are now well-established. Inner loyalty (2, above) required one to be reserved to avoid loss of dignity: here, one may safely show one's attachment openly. Consistency and undivided allegiance are required if one is not to allow oneself to be led astray.

5. *He holds together those who hold to him.*

Here, a ruler or influential man accepts those who come to him of their own volition. Those who do not come may go their own way unmolested. He invites none, flatters none: those who come do so freely, in voluntary dependence: opinions may be openly expressed. We should not woo favour. If a man cultivates the inner purity and strength necessary for leadership, then those meant for him will come of their own accord.

6. *One misses the right moment. Misfortune.*

If we go on hesitating to pledge ourselves, we shall regret it. If the beginning is not right, there is no hope of a right ending.

9

THE TAMING POWER OF THE GENTLE

≡≡ above THE GENTLE, WIND

≡≡ below THE CREATIVE, HEAVEN

THE CONDITION

The wind blows across heaven: the power of gentleness, restraining and taming.

The wind gathers the clouds, the rising breath of The Creative. It makes them grow great, but lacks the power to turn them to rain.

The hexagram represents a time when great clouds bring the promise of moisture and blessing to the land; but no rain falls.

When the strong is temporarily held in leash by the weak, only by gentleness can the outcome be successful.

In human terms, it represents a servitor who gently restrains a domineering ruler.

THE JUDGMENT

The power of gentleness has success:
Although it can give no rain,
It drives and shapes great clouds.

We are reminded of the time in Chinese history when King Wên served in the court of the reigning tyrant, Chou Hsin. The time for action on a large scale had not yet arrived. King Wên could only keep the tyrant somewhat in check by gentle persuasion.

The situation is not unfavourable. There is the prospect of ultimate success, but there are still obstacles in the way and we can only take preparatory measures.

Only through the small means of friendly persuasion can we exert any influence. The time has not yet come for sweeping measures. However, we may be able, to a limited extent, to act as a restraining, subduing influence.

The trigrams' attributes, inner strength with outer gentleness show us the way. To carry out our purpose we need firm determination within and gentleness and adaptability in external relations.

THE IMAGE

As the gentle wind shapes the clouds,
So the wise man refines his bearing.

The wind can indeed drive together the clouds in the sky; yet, being nothing but air, without solid body, it does not produce great or lasting effects.

So also, in times when one can produce no great effect in the outer world, one should seek to shape the expression of one's being in small ways: one should seek to refine the outward aspect of one's nature.

18

DEGREES OF CHANGE

1. *To return to one's station is no mistake.*
It lies in the nature of a strong man to press forward. But he encounters obstructions so he returns to the way suited to his situation, where he is free to advance or to retreat. This bodes well for it is wise and reasonable not to resort to force.

2. *One allows oneself to be drawn back.*
   Thus, does one not lose oneself.
One would like to press forward, but one sees from the example of others that the way is blocked. To push forward is not in harmony with the time. A reasonable and resolute man will not expose himself to personal rebuff but retreat with others of like mind. Thus, he does not needlessly endanger himself. His retreat is without struggle.

3. *Forcible advance. Failure and contention.*
One attempts to press forward forcibly, thinking that the obstructing power is slight. But since, here, the power lies with the weak, this sudden offensive is doomed to failure. Fate hinders the advance. But still one does not take the hint. One expected an easy victory but suffers a rebuff and compromises one's dignity.

4. *If one is sincere, danger vanishes.*
One is in the difficult, indeed, dangerous position of counsellor to a powerful man. One should restrain him so that right may prevail. Despite the danger, the power of disinterested truth carries such weight that the end is achieved. In this way does danger vanish and fear give way. No blame.

5. *If you are sincere and loyal*
   Then you are rich in your neighbour.
In firm attachments each partner complements the other: in the weaker person, loyalty: in the stronger, trustworthiness. Such mutual reinforcement leads to true wealth: not selfishly hoarded but shared. In this way is one rich indeed for one is not alone in one's riches. Pleasure shared is pleasure doubled.

6. *Success secured bit by bit. Be cautious.*
When success is at hand: the culmination of small effects produced by reverence for a wise man, great caution is required. To vaunt one's success would lead to danger; to presume upon it, a dangerous illusion. After the moon has waxed, its waning is inevitable. Be content with what has been achieved. To go on, before the right time, brings ill.

10

CONDUCT (COMPORTMENT)

≡ above   THE CREATIVE, HEAVEN
≡ below   THE JOYOUS, LAKE

THE CONDITION

The hexagram concerns comportment: the right way of conducting oneself.

The two trigrams can be understood, in family terms, as the relationship between a father and his joyous young daughter.

This shows the difference between high and low, upon which comportment, codes of correct social and moral conduct, depend.

The name of the hexagram in Chinese means 'treading' or 'treading upon something'. The small and cheerful follows and treads upon the large and strong. For the weak to take a stand against the strong is not, here, dangerous due to the inherent compatibility between the joyous and the strong.

That which treads correctly does not stay.

Conduct shows the basis of character: by being harmonious it attains its goal; it brings about harmonious conduct.

THE JUDGMENT

One treads upon the tail of a tiger.
It does not bite one. Success.

The situation is difficult. When the weak follows close to the strong it worries it. But the contact is in good humour and without presumption, so the strong takes it in good part and does not harm the weak.

If one is dealing with wild or intractable people, one should behave with decorum. Pleasant manners succeed even with irritable people.

THE IMAGE

Heaven above, lake below: discrimination.
Thus a wise ruler reassures his people.

Heaven and the lake show a difference of elevation that inheres in the nature of the two, hence no envy arises.

Among men there are necessarily differences of rank. It is impossible to bring about universal equality. But it is important that differences in social rank must not be arbitrary or unjust, for then envy and class struggle are inevitable. Only when rank corresponds with inner worth and inner worth forms the criterion of rank will the people accept it and order reign.

Therefore, let him who holds an honoured place beware. If he is strong, moderate and correct he conducts himself without blame.

DEGREES OF CHANGE

1. *Simple conduct. Progress without blame.*
By simple conduct we can remain free of social obligations. We can quietly follow our own way so long as we are content and make no demands on people. Inner strength guarantees progress. If one is content with simplicity, one can make good progress.

But if one is dissatisfied with lowliness, restless, and ambitious to advance; not to accomplish something worth while but only to escape from lowliness, then once one's purpose is achieved, one is sure to be arrogant and luxury-loving. Such progress is blameworthy. When a man is good at his work he is quite content to behave simply.

2. *Treading a smooth, level way. Persevere.*
He who withdraws inwardly from the bustle of life, seeks nothing and asks for nothing, is not dazzled by enticing goals. True to himself and unassailed, his path is level. He is content and does not challenge fate. Thus can one remain free of entanglements.

3. *A lame man can tread on a tiger's tail.*
   But the tiger will bite him. Danger.
   A one-eyed man can see. But clearly?
Here, inner weakness is combined with outwardly pressing forward. If, despite defects, a man considers himself strong he invites disaster. He goes beyond his strength. To be reckless, regardless of the adequacy of one's powers, is only rarely justified.

4. *If one is cautious and circumspect*
   One can tread on the tail of a tiger.
When inner power is combined with outer caution and hesitation, even dangerous enterprises succeed. Danger is overcome by progress with caution and circumspection.

5. *Resolute conduct. Persevere. Be wary.*
One's conduct must be resolute. But one must remain conscious of the danger connected with resoluteness, especially if it is to be persevered in. Only awareness of danger makes success possible. The right way is to be strong, moderate and correct.

6. *Review your conduct. Weigh its effects.*
One looks back over one's conduct to judge oneself. If its effects are good, one will be blessed. No one knows himself. It is only by the consequences of one's actions, by the fruits of one's labours, that one can judge what fortune one may expect. When everything is fulfilled, blessing will come.

11
PEACE (CONTENTMENT)

☷☰ above THE RECEPTIVE, EARTH
below THE CREATIVE, HEAVEN

THE CONDITION
Heaven within the earth represents peace. Heaven has placed itself beneath the earth.

When heaven and earth unite they are of one will: their influences are in harmony as, in spring, when the forces of nature combine and all living beings bloom and prosper and heaven itself seems to be on earth.

In the world of men, it is a time of social harmony. Those in high places show favour to the lowly and the lowly, in turn, are well-disposed towards the highly placed. Calm prevails. There is an end to all feuds. It is a time of union: of inter-relation.

STANDSTILL (12) is the inverse of PEACE: their natures are opposed to each other.

THE JUDGMENT
PEACE means union, inter-relation.
As the small departs, the great approaches.
Strength is within: the yielding is without.
In this way does each receive its due.

When the good elements in society are in control the evil elements come under their influence and change for the better.

When the spirit of heaven rules in man his animal nature comes under its influence and takes its appropriate place.

None of this occurs arbitrarily: it is born of the time: the season of spring in the course of the year and in the course of history: a time of favour and of success.

THE IMAGE
As heaven and earth unite in due season,
So the wise ruler divides and completes,
He furthers and regulates
The gifts of heaven and earth.
Thus does he aid his people.

Men divide the universal flow of time into seasons, according to the succession of natural phenomena. They mark off infinite space by the points of the compass. In this way is nature, in its overwhelming profusion of wonders, bounded and harnessed by man.

On the other hand, man adjusts to the right time and the right place the product of nature, to further her fruitfulness and to give increase to her yield.

This harnessing and yet furthering activity of man in his relationship to nature is the way by which nature rewards him.

DEGREES OF CHANGE

1. *Peace. One can direct one's will outward.*
   Inner affinities lead to undertakings.

In times of prosperity, every able man in public office draws like-minded people along with him. In such times, when it is possible to extend influence widely, the mind of an able man is set upon going out into life and accomplishing something.

2. *Forbearing; resolved; vigilant; impartial:*
   Thus can one find the way of the middle.

Here are four ways to overcome the hidden danger of laxity that lurks in times of peace and prosperity:

* By forbearance, greatness of soul, can one bear gently with the uncultured for, in the hand of a great man no one is unproductive.
* By resolution can one risk, if necessary, even dangerous undertakings.
* By vigilance and scrupulous action does one not overlook that which is distant.
* By impartiality does one avoid divisive factionalism and cliques.

3. *Enjoy good fortune whilst it lasts.*

Everything is subject to change. Prosperity is followed by decline. Evil can only be held in check; never abolished. But this should not make us sad. It should keep us mindful of the dangers and illusions of good fortune. So long as one's inner riches mean more to one than external fortune; so long as one remains inwardly superior to fate, then fortune will not desert one.

4. *He comes down to meet his neighbour:*
   Not boasting his wealth, but in sincerity.

In times of mutual confidence, people of high rank meet the lowly quite simply and without guile. This comes not from force of circumstances, but spontaneously and in accord with inner sentiment and conviction.

5. *A king's daughter marries. True modesty.*

A princess, though higher in rank than her husband, must yield to him like any other wife. Here we see the truly modest union of high and low. Herein is great blessing.

6. *Peace ends. Ruin is at hand. Withdraw.*

When the situation has begun to change for the worse, one should yield to fate, for to try to stave it off by violent resistance would only make one's collapse more complete, more humiliating. One should withdraw into one's own intimate circle and guard oneself in silence. The time must fulfil itself.

12
STANDSTILL (STAGNATION)

≡≡ above   THE CREATIVE, HEAVEN
☷   below   THE RECEPTIVE, EARTH

THE CONDITION
In contrast to PEACE (11), where heaven is below the earth, here heaven above draws further and further away from the earth which in turn, sinks down into the depths.

The movements of the trigrams diverge: the creative powers are not in relation.

It is a time of standstill and decline: just as, when high summer is past, autumnal decay sets in and all nature stagnates.

STANDSTILL is the inverse of PEACE: their natures are opposed to each other.

THE JUDGMENT
The great departs, the small approaches.
Evil people do not further a wise man,
So he withdraws and remains steadfast.

Although we are dealing with time conditions, the cause is, nevertheless, to be sought in the wrong course taken by man.

It is man who spoils things, aside from the cyclic course of nature.

Heaven and earth are out of communion. All things stagnate: they are benumbed. On earth confusion and disorder prevail. The dark is within; the light is without. The weak is within; harshness is without. The small waxes; the great wanes. Inferior people are rising; the wise are in decline.

But wise people do not allow themselves to be turned away from their principles. If the possibility of exerting influence is closed to them they nevertheless remain faithful to their principles and withdraw.

THE IMAGE
When heaven and earth do not unite,
The wise man turns to his inner worth.
He does not permit himself to be honoured.

When, owing to the influence of small men, mutual mistrust prevails in public life, fruitful activity is rendered impossible because its foundation is wrong.

The wise man knows what he must do under such circumstances. He must not allow himself to be dazzled by tempting offers to take part in public activities. This would only expose him to dangers.

He cannot assent to the meanness of others. He therefore hides his worth and withdraws into seclusion. He rejects rewards and stands aloof. Thus he escapes the dangers.

24

DEGREES OF CHANGE

1. *One withdraws to save one's self:*
   In steadfastness one finds blessing.

If it becomes impossible to make our influence count, only by retirement can we save ourselves from humiliation. But one succeeds in the highest sense by saving one's inner self. One may, by inner affinity, find friends in thus withdrawing.

2. *Standstill helps the great man:*
   He brings blessing, even to the small.

Small people flatter rank in a servile way. They would also serve the wise man if he put an end to their confusion, and thus do themselves good. But the wise man is calm, aloof, and does not mingle with the small. By his willingness to suffer personally he preserves his fundamental principles and so ensures their success. In this way standstill helps the great man win success.

3. *When small people come to bear shame,*
   This marks a turn for the better.

When inferior people, who have risen to power by cunning, do not feel equal to the responsibility they have taken upon themselves, they grow ashamed in their hearts. Even though it may not show, this is good.

4. *He who acts at the command of heaven*
   Is blessed. And so are those with him.

When standstill nears its point of change to its opposite, he who would restore order must feel himself called to the task and have the necessary authority. One who sets himself up according to his own judgment will make mistakes, be a failure. But one truly called is favoured by the time and those of like mind will share his blessing.

5. *As standstill gives way: great caution.*

The time changes. The right man to restore order is at hand. But such periods of transition are times for fear and trembling. Success is assured only through utmost caution. Ask always, 'What if it should fail?' Danger comes when one feels secure. Even in times of order one must never forget this.

6. *Effort brings standstill to its end.*

Standstill cannot last for ever, but it does not cease of its own accord. The right man is needed to end it. Peace and stagnation are quite different. Without continuous effort to maintain it, peace will change to stagnation. But stagnation will not change to peace without man's creative effort.

13
FELLOWSHIP

≡≡≡ above   THE CREATIVE, HEAVEN
≡≡≡ below   THE CLINGING, FIRE

THE CONDITION

In this hexagram it is the one yielding Yin line that holds together the strong. FELLOWSHIP is the complement of THE ARMY(7).

In THE ARMY one strong line uniting five weak lines reflects the character of a warlike army which, in order to hold together, needs one strong man to whom the others submit,

In FELLOWSHIP is reflected the character of the peaceful union of men which, in order to hold together, needs one yielding nature among many firm persons.

THE ARMY is represented by danger within; devotion, obedience, subordination, without.

FELLOWSHIP is represented by clarity, light-giving, within and strength without.

THE JUDGMENT

Fellowship in the open leads to success.
Great undertakings are favoured.
A steadfast, enlightened leader is needed.

As the sun shines upon all equally, so true fellowship among men must be based on a concern that is universal.

It is not the private interests of the individual that create lasting fellowship but, rather, the goals of humanity.

If such unity prevails, even great and dangerous tasks can be accomplished.

But to bring about this sort of fellowship needs a persevering and enlightened leader: a man with clear, convincing and inspiring aims with the strength to carry them out.

Clarity and order within is the essence of leadership: the way to culture. Only a great man can unite the wills of all under heaven by virtue of his inner clarity.

THE IMAGE

Heaven with fire: strength with clarity.
As the lights in heaven arrange time,
So the wise man organises society.

Just as the lights in the sky serve to divide and arrange time, so human society, like all things that belong together, should be organically arranged.

Fellowship should not be a mere commingling: that would be chaos, not fellowship.

For fellowship to be right, there must be organisation within diversity: clarity in purpose within the strength of diversity. Then does fellowship lead to order.

DEGREES OF CHANGE

1. *Open fellowship begins without the gate.*

The beginning of union among men should take place openly, outside the door, so that all are equally close to one another. No divergent aims have yet arisen. The basic principle of fellowship is equal accessibility to all concerned without self-interest or egotism or secret arrangements.

2. *Fellowship within cliques: Humiliation.*

Closed factions based on personal or egotistical interests originate from low motives and therefore lead, in due course, to humiliation. Exclusive factions, instead of welcoming all men, must condemn some to unite others.

3. *Fellowship that changes to mistrust.*

When men distrust each other they seek to spy on each other and lay traps. In their secret plotting, each suspects in his opponent the same wiles as in himself. Each tries to ferret them out. They depart further and further from true fellowship. They become more and more alienated. If a bad man seeks fellowship with a good man and resorts to cunning to stop the good from cultivating correct relationships with others, then his efforts will fail.

4. *Fellowship that comes forth from trouble,*
   For trouble brings one to one's senses.

After a quarrel comes reconciliation. Each confronts the other and, though obstacles remain, their trouble brings them to their senses. Their good fortune lies in their inability to fight. By getting into trouble they return to the right way.

5. *Men bound in fellowship weep then laugh.*
   First they struggle, then comes meeting.

Two men, outwardly separated but united in their inmost hearts, will struggle and grieve over obstructions between them. But it is by keeping true to each other that their sadness will be turned to joy. Confucius says of this:

   Life leads the thoughtful man on a path of many windings.
   Now the course is checked, now it runs straight again.
   Here winged thoughts may pour freely forth in words,
   There the heavy burden of knowledge must be shut away in silence.
   But when two people are at one in their inmost hearts,
   They shatter even the strength of iron or of bronze.
   And when two people understand each other in their inmost hearts,
   Their words are sweet and strong, like the fragrance of orchids.

6. *Fellowship among neighbours. No blame.*

The alliance of those who happen to live near each other lacks the real warmth of attachment that springs from the heart. Such fellowship still falls short of the ultimate ideal: the union of all mankind, the universal brotherhood of man. But we need not reproach ourselves if we join the community without separate aims of our own.

14
POSSESSION IN GREAT MEASURE

above THE CLINGING, FIRE

below THE CREATIVE, HEAVEN

THE CONDITION
The sun, the fire in heaven, shines upon everything. It brings both good and evil into the light of day.

The only yielding line in the hexagram occupies the place of honour and all the strong lines accord with it.

In the hexagram HOLDING TOGETHER (8), a strong man holds together subordinate persons: but here is represented a mild ruler who is surrounded by strong and able helpers.

It indicates a man of great inner wealth, in a position of authority, who is unselfish, modest and kind. Power is here expressing itself in a graceful and controlled way.

The trigrams' attributes combine inner strength with outer clarity: wealth indeed.

Ordinarily, accumulation of treasure brings disaster; but here it is not earthly, but heavenly, treasure that is being accumulated.

THE JUDGMENT
When strength and clarity unite:
A time of blessing: of strength within;
Of enlightenment and culture without.
The yielding receives the honoured place:
He is firm and strong, ordered and clear.

POSSESSION IN GREAT MEASURE is determined by fate and in accord with the time.

How can a yielding man have the power to hold fast and possess the strong? It is done by virtue of unselfish modesty.

A possession of this sort must be administered properly. Only by firmness and strength within can one show forth order and clarity.

The successful execution of measures demands that firm decision dwell within the mind, for only then can they be carried out with order and clarity.

All things come to him of high rank who is modest and kind.

THE IMAGE
As the sun sheds light on good and evil,
So the wise man curbs evil and furthers good.
He thereby fulfils the will of heaven.

As the sun exposes both good and evil, so men must combat evil and favour and promote the good. Only in this way does one obey the benevolent will of God who desires only good and not evil.

28

DEGREES OF CHANGE

1. *Keeping away from what is harmful;*
   Keeping mindful of difficulties to come.

When great possession is still in its beginnings, it can bring no blame since it has not yet been challenged, and there has been no opportunity to make mistakes. But many difficulties must yet be met. Only by remaining conscious of these can one stay inwardly free of possible arrogance.

2. *A big wagon will carry a heavy load:*
   A wise man relies on able helpers.

Great possession consists not only in the quantity of one's goods but, indispensibly, in their mobility and utility. Only then can they be used in great undertakings. One can load great responsibilities on to able helpers who give one their support and who are equal to their task. Thus is wealth made useful.

3. *A prince offers his wealth to heaven:*
   A wise man offers his to his prince.
   But a petty man cannot do this.

A magnanimous man should not regard his possessions as his alone but place them at the disposal of the ruler. Great goods can never endure as private property. A small man is harmed by great wealth.

4. *One is different from one's neighbour.*
   If one is poorer, one must shun envy;
   If one is richer, then possess modestly.

A poor man must shun envy and the temptation to vie with others. Thus does he avoid mistakes. On the other hand, a rich man should not rely upon his abundance. He avoids mistakes if he possesses modestly: as if he possessed nothing. Then is he truly rich.

5. *He who makes his truth accessible,*
   Yet is dignified, is favoured indeed.

People are won by unaffected sincerity, not by coercion. But benevolence alone, in making one's truth accessible, may lead to insolence. Such familiarity must be kept in bounds by dignity. In this way is confidence maintained; and then good fortune is assured.

6. *He is blessed by heaven. All goes well.*

In the fullness of riches and at the height of power, he who remains modest and honours the sage receives the beneficent influences of heaven. Heaven helps the man who is devoted; men help the man who is true. Thus, he who walks in truth and is devoted in his thinking is blessed by heaven. He has good fortune. There is nothing that does not further him.

15
MODESTY

≡≡ above THE RECEPTIVE, EARTH

≡≡ below KEEPING STILL, MOUNTAIN

THE CONDITION

The lowly earth, here exalted and placed above the mountain, represents modesty.

It shows how modesty functions in lowly, simple people. They are lifted up by it.

It shows how modesty functions in great and strong men. As the mountain dispenses the blessings of heaven in the clouds and rain that gather round its summit, and thereafter shines forth with heavenly light, so also, when a man of high rank is modest, he shines with the light of wisdom.

THE JUDGMENT

He who possesses something great
Must not make it too full.
Things are easy for the modest person.

By modesty can good character be made one's own. Modesty is ready to honour others and, in so doing, shines forth. Modesty is the attitude of mind that underlies sincere moral conduct. A modest man does not boast about his achievements.

It is the way of heaven to make empty what is full and to give increase to what is modest. When the sun reaches its zenith it begins to decline. When the moon is full, it wanes. But when the moon is empty of light, then does it begin to wax.

It is the way of the earth to change the full and augment the modest. High mountains become valleys; valleys become hills. Water wears down high places; it fills up the depths.

It is the way of men to hate arrogance and to love the modest. Powerful families draw down destruction upon themselves; modest ones become great. Modesty wins love: it cannot be passed by.

The way to expansion is by contraction: this is immutable law.

Man has it in his power to shape his fate for, according to his conduct, he draws upon himself good or evil influences.

THE IMAGE

Within the earth, a mountain. Inner wealth.
Thus, the wise ruler reduces fullness
And augments that which is too little.
He weighs things and makes them equable.

A wise ruler modifies the extremes that are the source of social discontent. Thus does he create equitable conditions.

DEGREES OF CHANGE

1. *A wise man is modest about his modesty.*
   And so can accomplish difficult things.

A wise man is lowly and so guards himself well. Any dangerous or difficult task is made easy if it is attended to directly and simply, unencumbered by claims and considerations to be taken into account. The unassuming nature of a modest man fits him to accomplish such enterprises. Where no claims are made, no resistances arise.

2. *Modest in heart: modest in manner.*

One's behaviour expresses one's inner self. When one is so modest that one's words and deeds express this, it brings one favour: one's capacity to influence others arises of itself. No one can stop it. Persevere.

3. *A man of merit who also is modest*
   Can carry things through to conclusion.

Fame is readily gained by great achievements. But if one allows oneself to be dazzled by fame, one will soon be criticised and difficulties will arise. If one stays modest, despite merit, one wins love and the support needed to carry things through.

4. *Modesty prompts action, not inaction.*

Even modesty in behaviour can be carried too far. Everything has its proper measure. Some officials shun prominence by hiding behind rules: they decline responsibility. This is the opposite of true modesty. It should be shown, in this case, by interest in one's work. Here, modesty should prompt action, movement, not inaction or inertia.

5. *Modesty expressed in forcefulness.*

Modesty must not be confused with a weak, good nature that lets things drift. A man of rank must resort, at times, to energetic measures, not to make an impression or to boost his rank but so as to be certain of those around him. He must be objective and in no way personally offensive. In this way is modesty made manifest even in severity.

6. *Modesty expressed in self-discipline.*

In adverse times the weak man will feel self-pity and lay blame on others, thinking it is modest not to defend himself. Not so. True modesty first seeks the disciplining of one's own ego and in one's immediate circle. Only by having the courage to turn one's forces against oneself can something forceful really be achieved.

16
ENTHUSIASM

☷☳ above THE AROUSING, THUNDER

below THE RECEPTIVE, EARTH

THE CONDITION

The trigrams' attributes are devotion within and movement without.

Enthusiasm is devotion in movement.

When a leader (the strong fourth line) meets with response from above and below, when his movement meets with devotion, it is the time of enthusiasm, carrying all with it.

This movement, along the line of least resistance, accords with the law of movement both in natural events and in human life.

THE JUDGMENT

ENTHUSIASM: movements of inherent harmony.

A great time indeed. One needs helpers.

An eminent man is at hand, in accord with the spirit of the people, who respond with willing devotion. To arouse enthusiasm, he must adjust himself to the character of those whom he has to lead: to find accord with the laws of movement and of nature.

These laws represent, not external forces but the inherent harmony of movements.

As heaven and earth move with devotion; as celestial bodies swerve not from their courses; as the seasons of nature accord with their times, so too, in human society, only such laws as are rooted in popular sentiment can be enforced. If they violate this sentiment, they only arouse resentment.

The secret of all natural and human law is movement that meets with devotion: that finds accord. Enthusiasm enables one to install helpers to complete even great undertakings without fear of secret opposition. It is by enthusiasm that one's will is done.

THE IMAGE

As thunder resounds out of the earth,

So kings of old made music in the temple

To honour merit and devote it to God.

A time for song and dance. A time for awe.

As summer begins, thunder comes forth to refresh nature and to resolve tension.

So too, music in sacred ceremonies brings joy and relief in song and dance. And, in solemn moments of religious inspiration, it refreshes and sanctifies the people.

In these rites is manifest the mystical bond between God and man: the summation of culture. He who wholly comprehends this has, as it were, the world spinning on his hand.

DEGREES OF CHANGE

1. *Enthusiasm that boasts. Misfortune.*
If one boasts enthusiastically of one's connections in high places, one invites misfortune. One is arrogant. Enthusiasm is justified only when it is a general feeling that unites one with others: never as an egotistical emotion. Be cautious, reserved.

2. *Be correct in a time of enthusiasm.*
   Persevere in inner steadfastness.
   To be ready to withdraw is prudent.
Whilst others are letting themselves be dazzled by enthusiasm, a wise man does not allow himself to be misled by illusions. He neither flatters those above nor neglects those below. He is as firm as a rock. He recognises, with great clarity, the signs of the times. At the first sign of discord he knows the right moment to withdraw, without delay. Thus is he self-reliant.

3. *Enthusiasm that looks upward. Regrets.*
   Hesitation can also bring remorse.
Enthusiastic looking up to a leader shows weakness, dependence, lack of self-reliance. Equally, one who hesitates too long will have regrets. One must seize the right moment if one is to do the right thing. Be self-reliant.

4. *The source of enthusiasm achieves much:*
   He gathers friends as hair in a clasp.
When a man is able to arouse enthusiasm by his own sureness and freedom from hesitation he attracts people because he has no doubts and is wholly sincere. By his confidence in them does he win their enthusiastic co-operation and so attain success. Thus is his will done. Like a hair clasp, he draws men together by the support he gives to them.

5. *Obstructed enthusiasm. Frustration.*
   Persistently ill: still he does not die.
Obstructed enthusiasm, a constant pressure, prevents one from breathing freely. But one is, at least, prevented from consuming oneself in empty enthusiasm. This kind of pressure can actually serve to keep one alive.

6. *Deluded enthusiasm. How can this last?*
   But to awake from delusion: no blame.
It is bad to let oneself be deluded by enthusiasm. But if this delusion has run its course, and one can still change, one is freed of error. A sober awakening from a false enthusiasm is always possible and very favourable. Deluded enthusiasm does not last: it is not a permanent condition.

17

FOLLOWING

≡≡ above   THE JOYOUS, LAKE

≡≡ below   THE AROUSING, THUNDER

THE CONDITION

Joy in movement induces following.

The trigrams' attributes unite movement with joyousness. Followers readily join a movement that is associated with joy.

When the strong (lower trigram) accepts subordination to the weak (upper trigram) the strong defers to the weak and shows consideration. In this way is the weak moved to follow the strong.

THE JUDGMENT

In following, be steadfast and consistent;
And if one would be one who is followed,
One must first follow in the right.

To obtain a following, one must first know how to adapt oneself. If a man would rule, he must first learn to serve. Only in this way can he secure from others the joyous assent necessary for them to follow him.

To obtain a following by force or cunning, by conspiracy or by creating factions, will arouse resistance and obstruct willing adherence.

Following tolerates no old prejudices.

But even joyous movement can lead to evil consequences. Hence, we are required to persevere and be consistent in doing right.

Just as one should not ask others to follow one unless this condition of rightness is fulfilled, so also, it is only under this same condition that we can, in turn, follow others without coming to harm.

THE IMAGE

As thunder withdraws to its winter rest,
So too, the wise man allows himself rest.
He follows and looks to the laws of nature.

In winter, thunder is not in motion but is withdrawn, at rest. It turns inward. Out of this image grows the idea of following by way of adaptation to the demands of the time: a time, here, for rest and recuperation.

Likewise, the wise man, after tireless activity all day, withdraws at night to allow himself rest and recuperation. He turns inward.

No situation can become favourable until one is able to adapt to it and not wear oneself out with mistaken resistance.

This idea, of obtaining a following by adaptation to the demands of the time, is truly profound.

DEGREES OF CHANGE

1. *As times change, one must adapt.*
   But one must not lose oneself. Persevere.

If one would lead others, one must remain responsive to the views of those who follow. But, at the same time, one must have firm principles so that one does not vacillate: following and concerning oneself only with matters of opinion. Once one is ready to listen to the opinions of others, one should not associate only with those who share one's views, but go out and mingle freely with all sorts of people: friend or foe. Only thus can one really achieve something.

2. *If one clings to thê weak,*
   One loses the strong.

In friendships one must make a careful choice. One can surround oneself with either good or bad company. One cannot have both at once. If one throws oneself away on unworthy and untrustworthy friends, one loses connection with the good, strong people with whom the good in oneself is furthered.

3. *If one clings to the strong,*
   One loses the weak.

When the right connections with good, strong people have been found, a certain loss naturally ensues. But one must part company with the inferior and the superficial. However, one will feel satisfied if one finds what one seeks and needs for self-development. One must remain firm, know what one wants, and not be led astray by passing whims.

4. *Followed by flatterers. Be sincere.*

A man of influence is often followed by false people seeking only personal advantage. To become accustomed to their flattery and fawning would bring misfortune. Only when a man is completely free from his ego and is sincere in his intentions does he acquire the clarity to see through such people.

5. *One follows the good with sincerity.*

Every man needs a lodestar, a guiding light. To follow, with conviction, the beautiful and good bring good fortune, of itself.

6. *A king's firm allegiance*
   Can bring back even the sage.

Here, an exalted sage who has already put the turmoil of the world behind him is drawn back into the world by the allegiance of the ruler that he may aid him in his work. In this way is the sage honoured: by being invited to share in the destiny of his ruler.

18
REMOVING CORRUPTION (DECAY)

above   KEEPING STILL, MOUNTAIN

below   THE GENTLE, WIND

THE CONDITION

The Chinese character for this hexagram represents a bowl in whose contents worms are breeding. The hexagram is concerned with inner conditions of corruption, decay.

It is the combination of the trigrams' attributes, gentle indifference within and rigid inertia without, that result in decay.

Guilt is implied. Hence the meaning of the hexagram is not simply 'What has been spoiled' but 'Work on what has been spoiled'.

We are enjoined to remove the cause of decay. It is not immutable fate that has caused the corruption, as in STANDSTILL (12), but rather the abuse of human freedom.

THE JUDGMENT

Removing corruption promises success.
If one deliberates with great care,
Before and after the starting point,
Then great undertakings are favoured.

We must first know the causes of corruption before we can do away with them. Hence, it is necessary to be cautious before starting.

Then we must see that the new way is safely entered upon so as to avoid a relapse. Hence, caution is necessary after starting.

Decisiveness and energy must replace the inertia and indifference that led to decay.

It is inner weakness, gentle, irresolute drifting, combined with outer inaction, inertia and rigidity, that lead to spoiling.

But it is the course of heaven that a new beginning follows every ending.

In removing corruption, let love prevail over both its beginning and its end.

THE IMAGE

As a wind, blowing low on a mountain,
Thus does the wise man remove corruption.
As a wind, he first stirs up the people.
As a mountain, he gives them nourishment.

Debasing attitudes and fashions corrupt human society like a turbulent wind that spoils growth. But the wise man works on what has been spoiled and renews society.

As a wind stirs everything, he first stirs up the people to remove stagnation.

Then, as a mountain gives tranquillity and nourishment to all that grows in its vicinity, he strengthens the spirits of the people and gives them peace.

36

DEGREES OF CHANGE

1. *Lay no blame upon one's forebears*
   In reforming what rigidity has spoiled.

Decay has been allowed to creep in by rigid adherence to tradition. But it is not yet deep-rooted. In remedying the decay one must attach no blame to one's forebears. One must not take such matters lightly. Only by keeping aware of the dangers connected with all reforms can they succeed in the end.

2. *In reforming what inner weakness has spoiled*
   One must not be too persistent.

When inner weakness has brought about decay, gentle consideration is called for in order not to wound. One must find the middle way. Do not proceed too drastically or persist to obstinate extremes. Be gentle.

3. *One reforms what has been spoiled:*
   A little remorse, but no great blame.

When one's reforms are a little too energetic minor discords will inevitably arise. But too much energy is better than too little. Although one has slight regret there is no serious blame. One's good intentions will compensate for minor mistakes.

4. *Tolerating decay leads to humiliation.*

If one is too weak to take measures against decay, rooted in the past but now beginning to manifest itself, then it will run its course and humiliation will result. One gains nothing by letting things drift.

5. *One sets things right with able helpers*
   And one's reforms meet with praise.

When one is confronted with corruption, originating from neglect in former times, one lacks the power to ward it off alone. But with able helpers, one can, at least, bring about a thorough reform correctly: with forbearance yet energetically. Even if one cannot create a new beginning such efforts are still praiseworthy.

6. *He serves not kings and princes;*
   The sage sets himself higher goals.

Not every man has an obligation to mingle in the affairs of the world. Some are developed to such a degree that they are justified in letting the world go its own way, refusing public office with a view to reforming it. But they have no right to sit idly and criticise. A sage withdraws in order to realise in himself the higher aims of man. He creates human values. He works not for one era, but for all people for all time.

19

APPROACH (BECOMING GREAT)

☷ above   THE RECEPTIVE, EARTH
☱ below   THE JOYOUS, LAKE

THE CONDITION

This hexagram means 'becoming great'. What becomes great are the two strong, light lines growing into the hexagram from within. The light-giving power expands with them.

The hexagram represents propitious time conditions as, after the winter solstice, when the light power begins to ascend again.

The meaning is further extended to include the idea of 'Approach'; especially the approach of the strong and highly placed in relation to what is lower.

APPROACH has the further meaning of the condescension of a man of high position towards the people and, in general, setting to work on affairs.

THE JUDGMENT

A time of joyous progress brings favour.
One should persevere in the right
For its end will surely come.

Spring is approaching. Joy and forbearance bring high and low nearer together. We must work with determination and perseverance to make full use of the propitiousness of the time.

But spring does not last forever: the light-giving influences will recede; the aspects will be reversed. We must take heed of this change in good time.

If we meet evil before it becomes a reality, before it has even begun to stir, then we can master it. But only by correctness and rectitude can success be assured.

THE IMAGE

As a lake is deep: as the earth is broad:
So is the wise man in his will to teach.

As a lake is inexhaustible in its depth, so is the sage inexhaustible in his readiness to teach mankind. As the earth is boundlessly wide, sustaining and caring for all creatures upon it, so is the sage without limits in his tolerance. He cares for and sustains all people: he excludes no part of humanity.

As a lake fructifies the earth with its inexhaustible moisture, so the sage fructifies man's inner being with his teaching.

NOTE: Whilst the first three DEGREES OF CHANGE concern the Approach, the rise to power, the last three show the Right Approach (attitude) of persons of higher rank towards those below.

38

DEGREES OF CHANGE

1. *Joint approach. Persevere in the right.*

As the good begins to prevail and to find response in influential circles, it is an incentive for men of ability. One should join the upward trend but not let oneself be carried away by the current of the time. To succeed, be steadfast in the right.

2. *Joint approach. A call from above.*

When one has the inner strength and the will to respond to a stimulus to approach that comes from above, one needs no admonition. One knows that all earthly things are transitory. One knows that a descent follows upon every rise. Such a one need not yield to fate. He will travel the paths of life swiftly, honestly and valiantly.

3. *An easy-going approach brings harm.*
   But if one is induced to regret it,
   Then one becomes free of blame.

When things go well for a man, he achieves power and influence. But in this lies the danger that he may relax, be over-confident, and allow an easy-going, careless mood to show itself. However, if he is induced to grieve over his mistaken attitude, and feel the responsibility of an influential position, then he becomes free of faults.

4. *The complete approach:*
   To draw up another with one.

Here is shown the open-minded approach of a person of high rank to a man of ability whom he draws into his own circle, regardless of his class. Both are thereby favoured.

5. *The wise approach.*
   This is right for a great prince.

A prince, or any leader, must have the wisdom to attract to himself people of ability who are expert in the directing of affairs. He must be wise, both in selecting them and in allowing them a free hand without interference from him. Only through such self-restraint will be found the experts needed to satisfy all of his requirements.

6. *The great-hearted approach.*
   The approach of a sage brings blessing.

A sage who has put the world behind him and withdrawn from life may, under certain circumstances, decide to return once more to worldly affairs and to approach other men. Thus does he bring great blessing to those he teaches and helps. Such great-hearted humility brings no blame to a sage.

20

CONTEMPLATION (VIEW)

≡≡ above THE GENTLE, WIND, WOOD
≡≡ below THE RECEPTIVE, EARTH

THE CONDITION
The shape of the hexagram reminds us of a type of tower, or viewing platform, characteristic of ancient China: a landmark that could be seen for miles around.

This gives the hexagram a double meaning. It means both contemplation (seeing) and also being seen, in the sense of being an example.

In human terms, the hexagram shows how a wise ruler contemplates the law of heaven above him and the ways of the people below and who, by good government, sets a lofty example for his people.

THE JUDGMENT
The ablution has been made
But not yet the offering.
Full of trust, they look up to him.

The sacred rites in ancient China began with an ablution, a cleansing, by which the Deity was invoked, after which an offering was made. The moment of time between these two ceremonies was the most sacred of all: the moment of deepest inner concentration.

If piety is sincere, expressive of real faith, the contemplation of it transforms and inspires all who witness it.

Likewise, in nature, the contemplation of the laws of the universe and their divine meaning gives, to the man called to a position of influence, the means of producing like effects. It is by the power of deepest inner concentration that religious contemplation develops in great men, strong in faith, that they apprehend the mysterious and divine laws of life and give expression to these laws in their own persons. In this way there emanates from them a hidden spiritual power that, of itself, influences others without their being aware of how it happens.

THE IMAGE
As the wind goes everywhere over the earth
And the grasses bend before its power;
So the wise ruler goes everywhere
And people are swayed, as grass by the wind.

A superior ruler goes everywhere, like the wind, to survey his realm. He penetrates the real sentiment of humanity and is not deceived. He impresses the people so profoundly, by his mere existence, that they are swayed by him, as is grass by the wind.

DEGREES OF CHANGE

1. *Childlike contemplation:*
   For the small man, no blame;
   For the wise man, humiliation.

When the influence of a wise ruler is not understood by common people, this matters little to them, for they will benefit from his actions whether they understand them or not. But for a wise man, contemplation without comprehension, the shallow, thoughtless view of prevailing forces, is a disgrace. He must contemplate them, as a connected whole, and try to understand them.

2. *Contemplation through one's doorway.*

One's view through one's doorway is limited: subjectively limited. It is egocentric. One tends to relate everything to oneself. One cannot put oneself in another's place and understand his motives. This may suit some, but, for a man in public life, such a narrow egotistical view is, of course, harmful.

3. *Self-contemplation: to decide one's way.*

At a point of transition, at a crossroads, self-contemplation means overcoming the naive egotism that sees everything from one's own standpoint. By reflection, one acquires objectivity. Self-knowledge is not self-preoccupation but, rather, concern about the effects one creates. It is only by the effects that our lives produce that we can judge whether we should advance or retreat.

4. *Contemplating the light of the kingdom.*
   He exerts influence as the king's guest.

When a man understands the secrets by which a kingdom can flourish he should be given authority. He should be, so to speak, a guest who is honoured and allowed to act independently. He should not be used as a tool.

5. *Self-contemplation: to judge oneself.*

One in authority, to whom others look up, must always be ready for self-examination: not idle brooding over oneself but examining the effects one produces. Only when these effects are good, and one's inner influences are good, can one be satisfied.

6. *The selfless contemplation of life.*

A sage, liberated from his ego, contemplates the laws of life rather than himself or his effects. He realises that knowing how to become free of blame is the highest good. He stands outside the affairs of the world. But he who has not yet forgotten the world, and still contemplates it, has not yet found peace.

21

BITING THROUGH (JUDGING)

≡≡ above   THE CLINGING, FIRE
≡≡ below   THE AROUSING, THUNDER

THE CONDITION

The hexagram represents an open mouth with an obstruction (the fourth line) between the teeth preventing the lips from meeting.

To bring them together it is necessary to bite energetically through the obstacle.

The trigrams for thunder and lightning indicate how, in nature, disturbing tension is energetically overcome by a storm.

Likewise, in human terms, the disturbances of harmonious social life, caused by criminals and slanderers, are overcome by recourse to criminal law and penalties.

THE JUDGMENT

Biting through has success
When unity cannot be established.

When an obstacle to union arises due to a tale-bearer and traitor who is blocking the way, permanent injury can be prevented by vigorous measures, taken at once. Deliberate obstruction of this sort does not vanish of its own accord: judgment and punishment are needed to deter or obviate it.

But it is important to proceed in the right way. The trigrams' attributes combine hardness and excitement with clarity and gentleness. Unqualified hardness would be too violent in meting out punishment: unqualified gentleness would be too weak. The two, together, create the just measure.

The man who makes such decisions should be yielding by nature, because gentleness prevents cruelty, but he must command respect by his conduct in his position. Thus is his gentle nature not turned into weakness.

THE IMAGE

Thunder and lightning: clarity and fear.
Thus kings of old made firm the laws
And clearly defined the penalties.

Clarity prevails when mild and severe penalties are clearly differentiated in accord with the nature of the crimes.

Clarity and severity together have the effect of instilling respect (not that penalties are ever ends in themselves).

Obstructions in social life increase when there is lack of clarity in the penal codes and slackness in executing them. The only way to strengthen the law is to make it clear and to make penalties certain and swift.

DEGREES OF CHANGE

1. *At first, a light punishment. No blame.*

The first time a man attempts to do wrong, the penalty should be a mild one, to prevent him from sinning further. Thus does he become free of blame. It is a warning to halt in time on the path of evil.

2. *Biting soft food, one buries one's nose:*
   In anger, one goes a little too far.

When it is easy to discriminate between right and wrong and one encounters a hardened sinner, one's anger is aroused: one's indignation blots out one's finer sensibilities (one's nose) and one is a little too severe. But there is no great harm in this because the penalty, as such, is just.

3. *To bite old meat; to lack authority;*
   Either will bring one some humiliation.

To persist in raising old issues (old meat) arouses hatred against oneself which puts one into a somewhat humiliating position. Equally, if one lacks the power to punish and culprits do not submit, it also brings one humiliation, in spite of punishment being right at the time. Here, lack of power allows decisions to hang fire indefinitely.

4. *Biting dry grisly meat: big obstacles.*
   Be as a metal arrow: hard and straight.

Here, great obstacles are to be overcome; powerful opponents need to be punished. Though this is arduous, one will succeed if one is hard as metal and as straight as an arrow. In this way can one surmount the difficulties. To know these difficulties and yet to remain steadfast brings favour indeed.

5. *Biting lean meat: clear but not easy.*
   Be like yellow gold: true but impartial.

This case is not easy but perfectly clear. It is because one is lenient by nature that one must be as true as gold and as impartial as yellow, the colour of the middle, the mean. In this way does one find what is appropriate. It is only by keeping aware of the dangers that grow out of one's responsibilities that one can avoid mistakes. Be wary. Be steadfast.

6. *He covers his ears with his own yoke:*
   He becomes deaf to warnings. Misfortune.

When a man is obstinate, incorrigible, and places himself arrogantly above justice, he does not heed just sentence passed upon him. Because of this he meets with the grave misfortune of being unable to hear justice even if he should wish to do so.

22

GRACE (ADORNMENT)

	above	KEEPING STILL, MOUNTAIN
	below	THE CLINGING, FIRE

THE CONDITION
Grace is represented by a fire breaking out of the secret depths of the earth. It blazes up to illuminate and beautify the mountain, the heavenly heights.

Grace, beauty of form, is necessary in any union for it to be well-ordered and pleasing and not disordered and chaotic.

THE JUDGMENT
Grace means adornment, beauty of form.
Graceful form is right in small matters.
Gracefulness, though pleasing, is not the essential or fundamental thing. It is only the external ornament and so must be used sparingly and only in little things.

In nature, the sun is the essential thing: the life of the world depends on it; but it is changed and given pleasing variety by the moon and the stars. By contemplating the heavenly forms we come to understand time and its changing demands.

In human affairs, graceful forms come into being when traditions exist that, strong and abiding like mountains, are made pleasing by a lucid beauty of form. By contemplating the social forms it becomes possible to shape the world.

Graceful, ordered forms in human life arise from the union of clarity and firmness in established rules of conduct.

Here are combined the light of love and the firmness of justice: love being the inner content and justice the outer form.

But whilst established rules suffice for application to everyday affairs, controversial issues require greater earnestness. Rules, though good in theory, can fail in practice.

THE IMAGE
Clarity within and quiet without:
The wise man has time for meditation.
The attributes, clarity within and quiet without, show tranquil beauty: the tranquillity of pure contemplation when desire is silenced, the will comes to rest, and the world-as-idea is revealed.

But contemplation alone will not put the will to rest absolutely. It will awaken again and then such perception will be seen as but a brief moment of exaltation. Even in this, one cannot find complete redemption.

DEGREES OF CHANGE

1. *One leaves the carriage and walks.*

It is more graceful to go on foot than to ride in a carriage under false pretences. A beginner, in a lowly place, must take upon himself the labour of advancing. Though an opportunity may come for one to ease one's way, a self-contained man will scorn help gained in a dubious fashion.

2. *He preens his beard.*
   It wags with his chin.

The beard is but an external ornament. It depends on, and moves only with, the chin. To devote care to it, for its own sake, without regard to the inner content of that which it adorns, would bespeak a certain vanity. External forms should be considered only as a result and attribute of content.

3. *He who has grace must still persevere.*

When one is, as it were, under the spell of grace, one's life is charmed and one's mood is mellow, as if induced by wine. Such grace can adorn, but it can also swamp one. Heed the warning. Do not sink into convivial indolence but be constant in perseverance. One's good fortune depends on this.

4. *Grace or simplicity? One must be true.*

When one has doubts as to which is the better, to pursue the grace of external brilliance or to return to simplicity, the doubt, in itself, implies the answer. At first, it may be disappointing to renounce the comforts one might have gained, yet one finds peace of mind in true relationships. Be warned of the danger of exaggerated grace. By excessive adornment, success exhausts itself.

5. *One seeks grace in the heights,*
   But one's gift is meagre. Humiliation.
   Yet if one is sincere one will be blessed.

A man withdraws from contact with people of the lowlands, who seek only magnificence and luxury, into the solitude of the heights. He finds one whom he respects and would like as a friend. But the gifts he has to offer are poor and few, and so, he feels ashamed. However, it is not the gift but his sincerity that counts. Thus does he find favour.

6. *Simple grace. No blame.*

At the highest stage of development all ornament is discarded. External form does not now hide content but brings out its full value. Perfect grace consists not in adornment, but in simple fitness of form.

23

SPLITTING APART (DISINTEGRATION)

≡≡ above KEEPING STILL, MOUNTAIN
≡≡ below THE RECEPTIVE, EARTH

THE CONDITION

The lines depict a house split apart. Only the roof has not, as yet, been split.

The dark Yin lines are mounting up to overthrow the last firm, light Yang line by exerting a disintegrating influence.

Dark, inferior forces overcome what is superior and strong not by direct means, but by undermining it gradually and imperceptibly, so that it finally collapses.

THE JUDGMENT

At a time of disintegration of the good,
The wise man undertakes nothing.

At a time when inferior people are pushing forward and are about to crowd out the few remaining strong and superior men, it is not favourable to undertake anything.

The right behaviour in adverse times is indicated by the trigrams' attributes: inner docility and devotion, and outward stillness.

The circumstances are due to the time. One should submit to the bad time and remain quiet. It is a question not of man's doing but of time conditions which, according to the law of heaven, show alternation of increase and decrease, fullness and emptiness.

As in autumn, when dark powers prevail, it is impossible to counteract the conditions of the time, so here, it is not cowardice, but wisdom, to submit and avoid action.

Fruit must, first, disintegrate and split apart before new seed can develop.

THE IMAGE

As a mountain rests, depends, on the earth,
So those above ensure their position
Only by giving generously to those below.

A mountain that is steep and narrow is lacking a broad base, and so, must topple. A mountain is strong only when it rises, out of the earth, broad and great; not proud and steep.

Likewise, those who rule must rest on, depend on, the broad foundation of the people. They should be generous and benevolent, like the earth that carries all.

Thus will they make their position as secure as the mountain, in its tranquillity.

Through generous giving, such as is the nature of the earth, an assured calm, as is the nature of the mountain, is attained.

DEGREES OF CHANGE

1. *Splitting apart begins from below.*
   Do not persist in open loyalty.

Inferior people are on the rise and begin their destructive burrowing, from below, to undermine the superior man's position. Those who remain openly loyal to the ruler are destroyed by slander and intrigue. The situation bodes disaster; even so, countermeasures are unwise. One must just wait.

2. *Splitting apart mounts upward. Danger.*
   Do not persist in proclaiming a view.

As the power of inferior people grows, so danger draws closer. One's rest is disturbed. One is isolated and without help from above or from below. One must adjust to the time to avoid the danger. Take extreme caution. Stubborn persistence in holding one's standpoint will lead to downfall.

3. *He splits from evil. Isolation. No blame.*

A man finds himself in an evil environment, to which he is committed by external ties. But he has an inner relationship with a superior man and thus attains the inner stability to free himself from the way of the inferior people around him. This will, of course, bring him into opposition with them, but that is not wrong. No blame.

4. *The splitting comes to one's own self.*

Here, misfortune is directly at hand. It has reached its peak. It can no longer be warded off. It must be endured.

5. *Forces are changed and favour comes.*

Here, in immediate proximity to the strong, light-giving Yang principle at the top, the nature of the dark forces undergoes a change. It no longer opposes the strong principle, by means of intrigue, but submits to guidance; as might a queen to her king, or as might a king to a sage. The submission is voluntary. In this way do all find favour.

6. *As fruit falls and splits to give new seed:*
   So good will arise, and evil be split apart.

When misfortune has spent itself, splitting apart reaches its end and better times return. It is from fruit that falls that come the seeds of the future, from which the good will sprout anew. Likewise, when the good man gains the support of the people, the evil man's wickedness is visited upon himself.

By the law of nature, evil destroys not only the good but also itself. It lives by negation: of itself, it is weak.

24

RETURN (THE TURNING POINT)

☷☳

above   THE RECEPTIVE, EARTH
below   THE AROUSING, THUNDER

THE CONDITION

The idea of a turning point arises from the entry into the hexagram, from within, of a strong, light line. As the winter solstice brings the return of the light so, in RETURN, the time of darkness and decay is past.

This turning point is part of a cyclic movement: not forced, but natural and spontaneous, in accord with the time.

THE JUDGMENT

Success comes in accord with the time.
Friends forgather in harmony. No blame.
Now is the time to undertake something.

The turning point is natural and, for this reason, the transformation of the old becomes easy. The old is discarded and the new is introduced. Both measures accord with the time and so no harm results.

Societies of people sharing the same view are formed openly, in harmony with the time. Selfish, separatist tendencies are excluded and so no mistake is made.

As is the course of nature, the course completes itself. It is not necessary to hasten anything artificially. In the relation of heaven and earth all things come at the appointed time. In RETURN we see the mind of heaven and earth: movement that develops within and acts through devotion.

In character formation, the return of the light principle counsels one to turn away from external confusions and back to one's inner light. It is in the depths of one's soul that one sees the Divine, the One. To know this One is to know oneself and one's place in the universe. This One is the ascending force of life in nature and in man.

THE IMAGE

As thunder withdraws to its deepest rest,
So kings of antiquity closed the passes;
Merchants and strangers did not go about;
Nor did the ruler travel the provinces.

The winter solstice is celebrated as a time of rest. Movement, the Arousing, is just beginning, so must be strengthened by rest and not prematurely dissipated.

Energy is renewed, reinforced, by rest.

As in the return of health after illness, or understanding after estrangement, all new beginnings must be treated with tender care.

DEGREES OF CHANGE

1. *Turn back early, before going too far.*
   Thus one finds not remorse, but favour.

Slight digressions from the good cannot be avoided. But one must turn back in time, before going too far. Especially in character development, every faintly evil thought must be put aside immediately before it takes root in the mind. Then is there no cause for remorse and all will go well.

2. *Quiet return, guided by a good man.*

Although return always calls for a decision, an act of self-mastery, it is made easier if one is in good company and can subordinate oneself to a good man. To bring oneself to put aside pride and to follow a good man is, surely, to find favour.

3. *Repeated returnings. Herein is danger.*

There are people of inner instability who feel a constant urge to reverse themselves. There is danger in côntinually deserting the good, because of uncontrolled desires, and then turning back again, because of a better resolution. However, this going back and forth does not lead to habituation in evil: one still wants to overcome the defect, which is good. Nevertheless, dangers are inherent within such circumstances.

4. *Whilst walking in the midst of others*
   One turns alone to follow the right way.

When one is in the society of inferior people but one's spiritual connections with a strong and good friend cause one to turn back alone, one's resolve to choose the good brings its own reward. One will surely find favour.

5. *Noble-hearted return. No remorse.*
   Thus does one test oneself.

When the time for turning comes, one must not evade it with trivial excuses but look within and examine oneself. If one has erred, one should make a noble-hearted resolve, a free decision, to confess one's faults. No one will ever regret having taken this road.

6. *Missing the turning point: Misfortune.*

In refusing to turn back, in defiantly seeking to attain one's objective by force, one incurs misfortune both from within and without, because one's attitude is wrong. This misfortune has its inner cause, so one loses, for a long time, all possibility of recovery. And he who rules others in this way is sure to encounter great set-backs. Blind obstinacy leads, inevitably, to judgment.

25
INNOCENCE

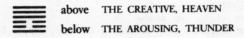 above THE CREATIVE, HEAVEN
below THE AROUSING, THUNDER

THE CONDITION
When one's inner movement follows and accords with the will of heaven, one is innocent and without guile. One's mind is natural and true, unshadowed by reflection or ulterior design. Where conscious purpose is to be seen, the truth and innocence of true nature have been lost. Nature not directed by the spirit is degenerate.

Innocence shows man's proper relationship to the divine: primal innocence in harmony with heavenly fate, the will of heaven.

THE JUDGMENT
Innocence succeeds through perseverance.
If one is not as one should be: misfortune.
When innocence is gone, where can one go?
Man has received from heaven a nature innately good to guide him in all his movements. By devotion to this divine spirit within, he attains an unsullied innocence that leads him to do right with instinctive sureness and without ulterior thought of reward and personal advantage.

But not everything instinctive is natural in this, its higher, sense but only that which is in accord with the will of heaven.

Without rightness, instinctive actions bring misfortune. When the will of heaven does not protect one, can one do anything?

When misfortune comes to the innocent it is of outer origin and will pass away. But when one's nature is not innocent, misfortune will follow of inner necessity.

Innocence depends on holding fast to heavenly virtue: being able to hold fast to heavenly virtue depends on innocence.

THE IMAGE
As thunder rolls under heaven,
And all things attain natural innocence,
So kings of old fostered all beings.
God comes forth in THE AROUSING: the Creative in movement. Thus begins all life.

In spring thunder, life energy, begins to move again under the heavens. All things sprout and grow. They receive, by the creative movement of nature, the primal innocence of their original state.

So too, a good ruler, in harmony with the time, draws upon the creative forces, the spiritual wealth, at his command, to foster all forms of life.

DEGREES OF CHANGE

1. *Innocent behaviour attains its will.*
The original impulses of the heart are always good, so one may follow them confidently, assured of good fortune and the achievement of one's aims. One thus attains one's goal with intuitive certainty.

2. *Count not on reaping whilst ploughing.*
   Thus should one undertake something.
One should do every task for its own sake as time and place demand and not with an eye to the result. Then each task turns out well and anything one undertakes succeeds.

3. *A passer-by takes one's tethered cow.*
Sometimes, undeserved misfortune befalls one at the hands of another. One's loss is another's gain. One's gentle, devoted nature is jeopardised.

   One must not be so naive as to presume innocence in others. In all transactions, however innocent, one must accommodate oneself to the demands of the time.

4. *He who can persevere remains blameless.*
We cannot lose what really belongs to us even if we throw it away. The divine spirit within can only be masked, not extinguished. Therefore we need have no anxiety. All that need concern us is that we should remain true to our own natures and not allow ourselves to be led astray by others.

5. *Take no medicine. One is not at fault.*
   The illness is from without:
   It will pass of itself.
An unexpected evil, innocently incurred, may come from without. If it does not originate in one's own nature or have a foothold there, one should not resort to external means to eradicate it, but quietly let nature take its course. Here, a man, by nature free of illness, vicariously takes on the ills of others and allows them to work themselves out in him. It will pass.

6. *When innocent action is wrong: wait.*
When, in a given situation, the time is not ripe for further progress, the best thing to do is to wait quietly. If one tries to push ahead in opposition to fate, success will not be achieved. Action without reflection brings the evil of bewilderment.

NOTE: The DEGREES OF CHANGE represent six time conditions. They favour, in turn:— intuitive arousal; action; circumspection; perseverance; passivity; and quiet waiting.

26

THE TAMING POWER OF THE GREAT

above   KEEPING STILL, MOUNTAIN

below   THE CREATIVE, HEAVEN

THE CONDITION

The image is of great power within, tamed by keeping still without: inner strength and outer stillness: the concept of holding firm.

Three aspects of the idea of 'holding firm' are expressed. Heaven within the mountain gives the idea of 'holding together'; Keeping Still restraining the Strong gives the idea of 'holding back'; and, thirdly, is the idea of holding in the sense of caring for and nourishing the worthy, as would a wise ruler in honouring and tending a sage.

THE JUDGMENT

> *To be able to keep strength still:*
> *This is great correctness.*
> *Firm and strong, genuine and true,*
> *Daily does a wise man renew his virtue.*
> *Thus can great things be undertaken.*

To hold firmly to great creative powers and to store them up, there is need of a strong, clear-headed man who is honoured by the ruler.

Through keeping still, the powers of character are so strengthened that a daily renewal takes place. Only through daily renewal, keeping still and collecting oneself, can one continue at the height of one's powers. Force of habit helps to keep order in quiet times, but in times when there is great storing up of energy, all depends on the power of personality.

However, since the worthy are honoured and, in this case, the strong personality is entrusted with the leadership by the ruler, it is favourable to enter public office; it is favourable to undertake great things.

He who so rules is in harmony with heaven, and so, even difficult undertakings succeed.

Thus does a wise ruler restrain strength within whilst also honouring merit.

THE IMAGE

> *Within the mountain: heaven. Hidden riches.*
> *So the wise man studies the sayings of old*
> *And the deeds of the past to enrich himself.*

In the words and deeds of the past lies hidden treasure that men may use to strengthen and elevate their own characters.

When a wise man studies the past, he enriches himself. He acquires not only mere knowledge but learns to apply it: thus he gives to the past a current reality.

DEGREES OF CHANGE

1. *Danger is at hand. One should desist.*
   Thus does one not endanger oneself.

When one wishes to make vigorous advance, but circumstances present an obstacle, one sees oneself held back firmly. Forcing an advance, here, would lead to misfortune. One should compose oneself and wait until an outlet is offered for the release of stored-up energies. In this way, one avoids the danger.

2. *When the restraining force overwhelms,*
   Remove the wheels from your wagon.

Here, there is no conflict between advance and restraint. The restraining force is absolutely superior, so no struggle takes place. One should submit and remove the wheels from one's wagon. In other words, content oneself with waiting. Thus is energy accumulated for vigorous advance later on.

3. *As good team horses pull together,*
   Go forward thus, aware of dangers.
   Practice both driving and self-defence.

When the way opens, and the hindrance is gone, one can go forward together with another man of strong will, acting in the same direction as one's own. But danger still threatens. One must remain aware of it or one will be robbed of one's firmness. One needs both the skill to go forward and also the skill to protect oneself against unforeseen attacks. It is good to have a goal, here, towards which to strive.

4. *The dehorning of a young bull. Success.*

A good way to restrain wild force is to forestall it. The horns of a young bull can be removed before they have even begun to be dangerous. Forestalling danger is the way to achieve an easy and great success.

5. *The tusk of a gelded boar. Good fortune.*

An impetuous forward drive can be restrained indirectly. A boar's tusk is, in itself, dangerous. But if a boar's nature is altered, and it is tamed, the tusk is no longer a menace. Wild force should not be combated directly but, instead, its roots eradicated. Good fortune comes from correct relations.

6. *One attains the way of heaven. Success.*

The time of obstruction is past. Energy, long dammed up, now forces its way out to achieve great success. Here is a sage, honoured by his ruler, whose principles now prevail and shape the world: a clear path ahead. This is the way in which truth works in the great.

27
PROVIDING NOURISHMENT

☶ above   KEEPING STILL, MOUNTAIN
    below   THE AROUSING, THUNDER

THE CONDITION
The shape of the hexagram depicts an open mouth, hence the idea of nourishment.

The upper trigram, like the upper jaw, keeps still; the lower trigram, like the lower jaw, has an upward movement.

PROVIDING NOURISHMENT represents the nourishment and care of oneself and also of others in a higher, spiritual sense.

WAITING (5) emphasises man's dependence on nourishment from heaven: here the emphasis is rather upon the human role in providing nourishment. The one is a process of nature: the other a process within society.

THE JUDGMENT
> *Pay heed to nourishing what is right*
> *And in what one seeks to nourish oneself.*
> *As heaven and earth nourish all beings,*
> *So a holy sage nourishes men of worth;*
> *And, thereby, reaches the whole people.*

In bestowing care and nourishment it is important that we nourish the right people and that we attend to our own nourishment in the right way, in harmony with what is right.

If we wish to know a man we have only to observe on whom he bestows his care and what sides of his nature he cultivates. The wise man does not injure the important for the sake of the unimportant, nor the superior for the sake of the inferior.

He who cultivates the lower parts of his nature is a small man: he who cultivates the higher parts of his nature is a wise man.

As nature nourishes all creatures, so the great man fosters superior men in order, through them, to nourish all men.

THE IMAGE
> *Within the calm mountain, thunder stirs.*
> *As God comes forth in THE AROUSING,*
> *And perfects in tranquil KEEPING STILL,*
> *So is the wise man, tranquil in movement.*

In spring thunder, life forces, stir and nature moves from within to care for all.

A wise man moves his jaw with care. He is careful of his words, that move from within. Likewise, is he temperate in his eating and drinking: that none exceed due measure. Thus does he care for and cultivate his character.

DEGREES OF CHANGE

1. *To envy others with drooping mouth,*
   Is to let go one's self-reliance.

One is fitted by nature and position to live freely and independently. If, instead, one looks with envy and discontent at others who are in better circumstances, then one invites derision and contempt. A drooping mouth cannot really be respected.

2. *To accept support brings misfortune,*
   If one deviates from self-reliance.

Normally, one either provides for oneself or is supported, in a proper way, by those whose duty and privilege it is to care for one. But if, due to weakness of spirit, one cannot support oneself and one accepts support as a favour, one shirks the right way; one becomes uneasy. This is unworthy, for one is deviating from one's true nature. This way brings ill.

3. *One turns away from true nourishment*
   To desire, to gratification, to desire . . .
   One's way runs round and round. No goal.

If one seeks nourishment that fails to nourish, one reels around from desire to gratification, back to desire and so on. Pursuit of pleasure to satisfy the senses brings one to no goal. No good comes of it.

4. *To accept support brings good fortune:*
   One seeks helpers like a hungry tiger.

In contrast to the man in DEGREE 2 (above), who was bent only on his own advantage, here a man of rank strives to let his light shine forth. But he needs helpers to attain his lofty aim so he seeks out the right people with the keenness and sharp eye of an insatiable tiger. It is because he is working not for himself, but for the good of all, that there is no wrong in such zeal.

5. *He deviates from self-reliance. Good.*
   But he should not undertake great things.

Here a ruler, who should be undertaking the nourishment of his people, is aware of his own deficiencies. So he must deviate from his accustomed path to seek out the sage. He must keep aware of his dependency, not push himself forward nor should he yet attempt too much.

6. *The sage who nourishes brings blessing.*

An honoured sage, whose influence nourishes all, is conscious of his heavy responsibility. If he remains aware of dangers, he may confidently undertake even great and difficult tasks for the good of all. Such works bring blessing for him and for all.

NOTE: THE DEGREES concern, first, nourishing oneself (1, 2 & 3); and then others (4, 5 & 6).

28

GREAT HEAVINESS

☱ above   THE JOYOUS, LAKE

☴ below   THE GENTLE, WIND, WOOD

THE CONDITION

The hexagram consists of four strong lines inside and two weak lines outside. When the strong are outside and the weak inside, all is well and there is nothing out of balance or extraordinary in the situation. Here the opposite is the case.

The image is of a beam, a ridgepole, that is thick and heavy in the middle and weak at the ends. It sags to breaking point because the ends are too weak for the load they bear.

The condition is extraordinary and cannot last. It must be changed, must pass, or misfortune will result.

THE JUDGMENT

The weight of the great is excessive:
The load too heavy; the support too weak.
At a time of Great Heaviness
It furthers one to have somewhere to go.

Movement that goes too far leads to overweighting. It is an exceptional time and situation, therefore extraordinary measures are demanded. We must find a way of transition as quickly as possible and take action.

Even though the time is unusual, the strong is in the middle, at the centre of gravity, and so a revolution need not be feared.

Nothing is to be achieved by force. The attribute of the inner trigram shows the way. The problem must be solved by gentle penetration to the meaning of the situation.

The change-over to the new conditions promises success, but it demands real superiority.

The time when greatness holds sway is truly a momentous time.

THE IMAGE

As a lake rises above the treetops
In extraordinary times of flood:
So the wise man, in extraordinary times,
Is unconcerned if he stands alone.
Even if he has to renounce the world,
He is as undaunted as joyousness.

When a lake rises over the treetops in a time of flood, the time is extraordinary and the condition is temporary.

The attitude proper to such exceptional times is to be as firmly rooted as the tree (the lower trigram), which endures even when it stands alone, and as undaunted as joy (the attribute of the upper trigram).

DEGREES OF CHANGE

1. *To spread rushes beneath is no mistake.*

To undertake something, in extraordinary times, requires extraordinary caution: just as, when setting down a heavy load, one takes care to put rushes under it, so that nothing will break. Rushes are, in themselves, worthless; yet they can have a very important effect. Exceptional enterprises cannot succeed without the utmost caution in the laying of their foundations.

2. *A dry poplar sprouts at the root.*
   An older man takes a young wife. New life.

Here we see an extraordinary reanimation of the processes of growth. Although unusual, such action bodes well. Just as an older man may marry, defer to, a girl of lowly rank, so also, in politics, in extraordinary times, one does well to join with the lowly, for this affords the possibility of renewal.

3. *The ridgepole sags to breaking point.*

If one obstinately insists on pushing ahead, accepting no advice from others, one will receive no support. Thus does one's burden grow to breaking point. To plunge wilfully ahead, in times of danger, only hastens the catastrophe. One's obstinacy has cut one off from all possibility of support.

4. *The ridgepole is braced. Good fortune.*
   But any ulterior motives bring shame.

Through friendships with people of lower rank, a responsible man succeeds in mastering the situation. But if, instead of working to rescue the whole, he were to misuse his connections, to obtain personal power and success, it would lead to humiliation.

5. *A withered poplar puts forth flowers.*
   A man takes an older wife. No renewal.

A withered poplar that puts forth flowers only exhausts its energies and hastens its end. An older woman will remain barren and so no renewal will take place. In politics, in times of insecurity, if we give up alliance with those below, and keep only to those of higher rank, then an unstable situation is created. No blame. No praise.

6. *Swamped by circumstances. But no blame.*

When the unusual situation reaches a climax, and one's courage and intention lead one inevitably to danger and misfortune, one incurs no blame, even in giving up one's life, that the good and the right may prevail. There are things more important than life.

29

THE ABYSMAL

≡≡ above   THE ABYSMAL, WATER
≡≡ below   THE ABYSMAL, WATER

THE CONDITION

THE ABYSMAL means plunging in, danger. In the trigram, here doubled, a light Yang line has, as it were, plunged in between two dark Yin lines and is closed in by them as is water closed in by a ravine.

Water comes as a heavenly gift from above. It is placed within the earth and gives rise to all life upon earth.

Applied to man, THE ABYSMAL represents his deepest core, his soul locked within his body: the light force enclosed within.

Danger, here, is an objective situation we must adjust to; not a subjective attitude. When danger originates from within, it means either foolishness or guile. Here, the danger is external and we can escape it, like water from a ravine, if we behave correctly.

THE JUDGMENT

> *When danger is doubled, be true, sincere.*
> *He that is so, has success in his heart.*

Water shows us the right way in danger. Water flows on and on. Water fills up deep places. It shrinks not from any danger nor from any plunge. But nothing can make it lose its essential nature. It remains true to itself under all conditions.

Likewise, be sincere, correct in conduct, when confronted by difficulties. Thus can one penetrate the meaning of the time. From gaining inner mastery of a problem flows, naturally, action that leads to success.

Do what must be done with thoroughness. Go forward. Do not tarry in danger.

But, properly used, danger also protects. Heaven is protected by its perilous height; and nations by mountains and waters. Rulers use danger to protect against foes from without and against turmoil within. But never can danger be justified as an end in itself.

THE IMAGE

> *As water flows on, on, on to reach its goal,*
> *So the wise man walks in lasting virtue.*

Water fills every depression before it flows on. Thus does a wise man foster the good in his own nature. In his teaching, he is like water: consistent and dependable. He is true to himself under all circumstances. He escapes being engulfed by desires and passions by holding firm to the good within.

DEGREES OF CHANGE

1. *Repeated danger. One falls into a pit,*
   because one has lost the way.

By growing used to what is dangerous one can easily allow it to become part of one. By familiarity with danger one grows used to evil. Being weak, one does not have the inner strength to withstand such temptation. Thus does one lose the right way and misfortune is the natural result.

2. *In danger, strive for small things only.*

When one is in danger, one ought not to attempt to get out of it immediately, regardless of the consequences. At first, one must content oneself with not being overcome by it. Do not seek the impossible. Remain calm. Adapt to circumstances. Weigh the conditions of the time. Be satisfied with small gains. A spring flows only slowly at first. It tarries a while before making its way into the open.

3. *Forward and backward. Abyss on abyss.*
   When in a bog, pause at first and wait.

Danger without, disquiet within. Every step, forward or backward, leads into danger. Here, escape is out of the question. One must not be misled into action: that would only bog one down deeper in the danger. Although disagreeable to remain so, one must wait until a way out shows itself.

4. *In lowly earthen vessels: wine and rice,*
   presented most simply. No blame in this.

In times of danger ceremonious forms are dropped. What matters most is sincerity. Although customary, for one who would serve, to come bearing gifts, here everything is simplified to the utmost. Even though one has no sponsor, and one's gifts are meagre, yet it is one's honest intention, of mutual help in danger, that prevents humiliation.

5. *Water fills an abyss, only to the rim.*

Danger comes if one is too ambitious. Water does not pile up in a ravine but rises only to the rim's lowest point to escape and flow on. Be likewise. Is it not enough merely to extricate oneself from the danger? Great labours cannot succeed in dangerous times.

6. *Shut in by thorn-hedged prison walls;*
   For years one does not find the way.

Extreme danger. One has lost the right way. One is so entangled by sin, one has no prospect of escape. Shackled and imprisoned, one must, as it were, serve one's sentence.

30
THE CLINGING

≡≡ above THE CLINGING, FIRE
≡≡ below THE CLINGING, FIRE

THE CONDITION
In the trigram, THE CLINGING, here doubled, a dark line clings to two light lines, whereby the light lines are made bright.

THE CLINGING means 'clinging to something', 'being conditioned', 'depending or resting upon something'. It also means 'brightness'.

The image of THE CLINGING is fire. Fire has no definite form but clings to the burning object and is thus bright.

THE CLINGING also stands for nature in its radiance. Its attribute is clarity.

THE JUDGMENT
One can succeed only by perseverence.
The care of one's cow brings one favour.

What is dark, weak, dependent, clings to what is light and strong and so enhances the brightness of the latter. That which gives out light must have within itself something that perseveres, otherwise it will burn itself out. All that gives light is dependent upon something to which it clings so that it may continue to shine.

As the sun and moon cling to heaven and as grass and trees cling to the earth, so the dedicated man clings to what is right. By his twofold clarity, both within and without, he can shape the world.

For one's nature to be transfigured, one must cling to the forces of spiritual life. Human life is conditioned and limited. Before one can achieve success, one must accept these limitations and make oneself dependent upon the harmonious and beneficent forces of the cosmos. Only by cultivating, within oneself, a cowlike docility, in an attitude of compliance and voluntary dependence, can one acquire clarity without sharpness or arrogance and find one's place in the world.

THE IMAGE
The great man perpetuates his brightness
And illumines all quarters of the world.

The double trigram represents the sun's repeated movement: light that endures.

As the sun illumines all things on earth, so, by the clarity of his nature, the great man causes light to spread ever wider and to penetrate ever more deeply into the nature of man. Thus does he continue and further the work of nature in the human world.

DEGREES OF CHANGE

1. *At sunrise one's thoughts run crisscross.*
At dawn one's mind awakes and begins again its connections with the world. One's thoughts run crisscross. Activity and haste prevail. But one must preserve inner composure and not allow oneself to be swept along in the bustle of life. Thus does one acquire the clarity of mind to come to terms with the innumerable impressions that pour in. Beginnings hold the seeds of what is to follow. Therefore, it is precisely at the beginning that serious concentration is important.

2. *The yellow light of midday. Blessing.*
Yellow, the colour of measure, moderation and mean, is the symbol of the highest art and culture. Consummate harmony consists in holding to the mean, the middle way.

3. *At sunset, men either feast and sing,*
   Or bewail the shortness of life. Misfortune.
Sunset reminds us that life is transitory and conditional. Caught in this eternal bondage, most are robbed also of their inner freedom. They tend either to revelry, to enjoy life whilst it lasts, or yield to melancholy and spoil the precious time by lamenting old age. Both are wrong. To a wise man, it matters not whether death comes early or late. He cultivates himself and bides his time. In this way does he secure his fate.

4. *A meteor is bright, but soon is gone.*
   A straw fire flares quickly, but soon dies.
Fire clings to wood, but it also consumes it. Clarity of mind is rooted in life, but it can also consume one's life. He who is excitable and restless may quickly rise to prominence, but he will produce no lasting effects. It is bad to spend oneself too rapidly.

5. *Tears and sighs. But lament brings blessing.*
At the zenith of one's life is the time to understand the vanity of all things, to put aside hope and fear. If one is intent upon retaining clarity of mind, one's grief will bring one favour. It is not a passing mood but a real change of heart. Blessing comes not from arrogance but from humility.

6. *True enlightenment: measured discipline.*
In shaping oneself to remove the evil, one should root out bad habits but tolerate those that are harmless. To remove evil in political life, one roots out the leaders but spares the followers. Asceticism that is too strict, like undue severity, fails in its purpose.

31

INFLUENCE (WOOING)

≡≡ above   THE JOYOUS, LAKE
    below   KEEPING STILL, MOUNTAIN

THE CONDITION

Strength and stillness within - a quiet, persistent influence - here find a cheerful and joyous response from without. This gives the idea of influence or stimulation.

In courtship, the male woos. The masculine principle takes the initiative and subordinates itself to the female principle.

It is by natural affinity that each influences, and is influenced by, the other.

The bases of all social relationships are in WOOING, MARRIAGE (32) and THE FAMILY (37).

THE JUDGMENT

Influence succeeds by perseverance.
To take a maiden to wife brings favour.
To defer to the weaker brings peace.

When the strong places itself below the weak they unite. All successful union depends on the effect of mutual attraction.

By keeping still within, whilst experiencing joy without, one can prevent joy from going to excess and hold it within proper bounds.

It is steadfastness that makes the difference between seduction and courtship, for in courtship the stronger defers to the weaker and shows consideration.

In this attraction between affinities, we see a general law of nature:

* Heaven and earth attract each other to bring all creatures into being.
* By attraction does the sage influence men's hearts so that the world attains peace.

We can learn the nature of all beings in heaven and earth by the attractions they exert. By contemplating their outgoing, stimulating influences can we know them.

THE IMAGE

At the top of the mountain, a lake.
Thus is the wise man ready to receive
By virtue of his emptiness.

As land is stimulated and enriched by the moisture of a lake, so a wise man stimulates the hearts of men by his receptivity.

A lake at the summit of a mountain does not jut out as a peak but lies sunken. Thus does the wise man keep his mind humble and free, so that it may remain receptive to good advice.

People soon give up counselling, or taking counsel from, a man who thinks he knows everything better than anyone else.

DEGREES OF CHANGE

1. *The inner stimulus to influence.*
When the idea of influence has come into being, it is not, at first, immediately apparent to others. As yet, only the will is directed outwards. Whilst one's intentions have no visible effect, it is of no importance to the outside world and so leads neither to good nor to evil.

2. *Dependent influence bodes ill. Wait.*
When the movement to influence is not self-governed, it invites misfortune. One should wait quietly until one is impelled to action by a real influence. By tarrying thus one can keep oneself free of injury.

3. *Influence that conforms to its following.*
    To continue this way is humiliating.
Every mood of the heart is a stimulus to movement. But to pursue every desire, or to act on the spur of every caprice, is wrong. One makes oneself contemptible by directing one's will to baser things.

   Three considerations are suggested:
* A wise man does not run headlong after all those whom he would like to influence but will hold back in certain circumstances.
* Nor does he yield immediately to every whim of those in whose service he stands.
* And, concerning the impulses of his own heart, he never ignores self-inhibition, for this is the basis of human freedom.

4. *Persevere in the good. Remorse will pass.*
    But if one strains, few will follow.
By steadfastness, one's inner influences will be constant and good, bringing no cause for regret. When quiet inner power is at work, one's influence and effects are right. But to strive to influence others, by manipulation, brings stress and exhaustion. An agitated mind has no clear light. Moreover, striving limits one's influence: few will follow.

5. *Influence with a firm will: no confusion.*
    Influence with a stiff neck: no effect.
Good influence stems from the calm of inner balance: a will not rigid, but firm: that weighs ramifications and details. It is will-power that controls all stimuli from within or without. Avoid rigidity: if one cannot be influenced, how can one influence others?

6. *The influence of a wagging tongue*
The most superficial way to try to influence others is through empty talk. Such chatter, necessarily, remains insignificant.

32

DURATION (MARRIAGE)

above   THE AROUSING, THUNDER

below   THE GENTLE, WIND

THE CONDITION

Thunder and wind are constantly paired phenomena. Their union is enduring.

In the sphere of human relationships the hexagram represents the institution of marriage: the enduring union of the sexes. The husband is the directing and moving force outside whilst the wife, within, is gentle and devoted.

DURATION is the union of inner gentleness and outward movement.

DURATION means that which always is.

THE JUDGMENT

DURATION is continuity in change.

DURATION succeeds through self-renewal.

Duration is a state whose movement is not worn down by hindrances. It does not rest, for mere standstill is regression, but is, rather, the self-contained and self-renewing movement of an organised, firmly integrated whole: in accord with immutable laws and beginning anew at every ending.

Each end is reached by inhalation, contraction: an inward movement. It becomes a new beginning in exhalation, expansion: where the movement is directed outwards.

Heavenly bodies exemplify duration. They wax and wane in fixed orbits and, because of this, their light-giving power endures.

The seasons of the year follow fixed laws of change and transformation. Thus can they produce effects that endure.

So, likewise, the dedicated man embodies an enduring meaning in his way of life. Duration brings about unity of character.

THE IMAGE

As thunder and wind: mobile yet enduring:

Thus does the wise man stand firm.

Thunder rolls and the wind blows. Both are examples of extreme mobility and seem the very opposite of duration. But the laws endure, that govern their coming and their going.

Likewise, the wise man stands firm: he does not change his direction. His independence is not based on rigidity and immobility of character: he always keeps abreast of the time and changes with it. What endures is the unswerving directive, the inner law of his being, which serves to determine all his actions. A firm man can adapt himself.

DEGREES OF CHANGE

1. *Seeking duration too hastily, one fails.*
   To want too much immediately is wrong.

Whatever endures can be created, only gradually, by long-continued work and careful reflection. If we wish to compress something we must first let it fully expand. He who demands too much at once acts precipitately. Because he attempts too much, he ends by succeeding in nothing.

2. *As inner strength comes, remorse goes.*

When one's inner force of character is greater than one's outward power, one may fear attempting something beyond one's strength: overstepping the limits of moderation. But it is by control of inner strength that excess is avoided. Fear not.

3. *Without duration in one's character,*
   Disgrace and persistent humiliation.

If one remains at the mercy of hopes and fears aroused by the outer world, one will lose one's inner consistency of character. Distressing experiences, often from an unforeseen quarter, are evoked, not least, by one's own excited, superficial nature.

4. *Duration in character is not enough.*
   Persistence in search is not enough.

He who persists in stalking game where there is none may seek for ever and find nothing. What is not sought in the right way, in the right place, cannot be found.

5. *Duration acquired through following*
   Brings good fortune to a wife,
   But misfortune to a husband.

A wife should perseveringly follow her man her whole life long. But a man should, at all times, hold to what is his duty at the given moment. It is right for a wife to hold conservatively to tradition. But a man must always be flexible, adaptable, and allow himself to be guided solely by what his duty requires of him.

6. *Enduring restlessness is harmful.*

There are people who live in a state of perpetual hurry, never attaining inner composure. Restlessness prevents thoroughness. It is dangerous, if dominant, in places of authority. Movement that cannot control itself will fall prey to restlessness. It is harmful. It is not in accord with the time.

In the first DEGREE OF CHANGE, movement was too hasty to endure. Here, the movement endures, but accomplishes nothing.

33
RETREAT (WITHDRAWAL)

▤ above   THE CREATIVE, HEAVEN
     below   KEEPING STILL, MOUNTAIN

THE CONDITION
Two dark Yin lines have entered the hexagram from below. When the power of the dark ascends, the light retreats to security so that the dark cannot encroach upon it.

This retreat is not a matter of man's will but of natural law, as in late summer, when the forces of winter are already beginning to show their influence.

Therefore, in this case, withdrawal is proper: it is the correct way to behave so as not to exhaust oneself.

Retreat is not the flight of a weak person but the voluntary withdrawal of a strong one. Flight means saving oneself at all costs: retreat is a sign of strength.

THE JUDGMENT
Seek success only in small matters.
Persevere thus, in accord with the time.
Success lies in being able to retreat at the right time and in the right way.

Strength is shown not in attempting to force anything but by perseverance only in small matters. We must not miss the right moment for retreat whilst we are in full possession of power and position.

By being able to interpret the signs of the time, before it is too late, we can retreat rather than be drawn into a desperate struggle.

To retreat is not to abandon the field to the opponent but to make it difficult for him by persevering resistance in small things.

Thus do we prepare, in retreating, for the counter-movement.

Understanding the laws of constructive retreat is not easy. The meaning that lies hidden in such a time is important.

THE IMAGE
As heaven retreats before the mountain,
Thus does the wise man keep his distance.
However high a mountain rises towards heaven, heaven retreats before it; remains out of reach. So also should a wise man retreat into his own thoughts as small men come forward. He does not hate the small, for hatred is a form of subjective involvement that binds one to the hated object.

The wise man shows his strength (heaven's attribute) by bringing the small to a standstill by his dignified reserve.

DEGREES OF CHANGE

1. *At the tail-end of retreat: Danger;*
   Keep still. Do not even wish to act.

To be at the tail-end of a retreating movement, one is dangerously exposed to the pursuing enemy. It is better to be at the front in retreat. Keeping still is the best way of escaping from the danger.

2. *Hold fast to the right by force of will.*
   So none can tear one loose.

One may find oneself in the position of the smaller man from whom, it seems, the wiser man is retreating. But if one's quest is right and one is correct, in line with duty, and one is strong in purpose then, by perseverence will one reach one's goal.

3. *A halted retreat is nerve-racking.*
   Retain only those who cling to one:
   A good act. But not for great ends.

When retreating it is both unpleasant and dangerous to be held back. It impedes one's freedom of action and brings fatigue. One should retain only those who refuse to let go so that, at least, one can keep the initiative and not fall helplessly under their control. Even so, the situation is far from satisfactory. One may thus avoid the immediate danger, but what can one hope to accomplish with such people?

4. *Voluntary retreat brings favour,*
   But, to the small man, downfall.

In retreating, the wise man's intent is a willing, friendly departure. He adjusts his mind and does not violate his convictions. But the small man suffers and degenerates when deprived of wiser guidance. He is harmed because he cannot rule himself.

5. *Friendly retreat. Persevere, firm in will.*
   Do not be led astray by side issues.

The wise man will recognise in time the moment for retreat. Thus is his retreat friendly, not disagreeable. Yet, for all his observance of form, absolute firmness of decision is necessary to avoid being led astray by irrelevant considerations.

One may, equally, retreat inwardly, whilst still at one's post, and prepare for return.

6. *Cheerful retreat. One has no doubts.*

One knows exactly what to do. One has no doubts. Inner detachment is established. One is free to depart. To see clearly ahead frees one of doubt and brings one cheer. Such a clear path ahead leads to the good.

34

THE POWER OF THE GREAT

above THE AROUSING, THUNDER

below THE CREATIVE, HEAVEN

THE CONDITION

Four light lines, strong and great and powerful, have entered the hexagram from within and are about to ascend higher.

The trigrams' attributes unite strength within and movement without.

THE POWER OF THE GREAT means a time when the great are powerful.

THE JUDGMENT

Strength in movement: the basis of power.
But greatness is nothing without rightness.

The hexagram represents a time when inner worth mounts with great strength and comes to power.

But its strength has already passed beyond mid-way, hence there is the danger that one may rely entirely on one's own power and forget to ask what is right.

There is also the danger that, being intent on movement, one may advance too soon. Therefore, perseverance is essential.

Truly great power does not degenerate into mere force but remains inwardly united with the fundamental principles of right and of justice. When we understand this point, namely, that greatness and rightness are indissolubly united, we understand the relations of heaven and earth and the principles of fate.

Strong in movement. This union of strength and movement is the basis of power:

* inner strength makes it possible to master the egotism of the sensual drives;
* movement makes it possible to execute the firm decision of the will.

Greatness and rightness are not two different things: without rightness there is no greatness.

Greatness of power shows itself in the fact that one pauses.

THE IMAGE

As thunder moves in accord with heaven,
So too, the wise man accords with the right.

As thunder in movement accords with the movement of heaven, producing great power, so too, the wise man does not tread upon paths that do not accord with established order.

True greatness depends upon being in harmony with what is right. In times of great power the wise man avoids doing anything that is not in harmony with what is right.

DEGREES OF CHANGE

1. *Advancing by force brings misfortune.*

Great power in a lowly situation is inclined to effect advance by force. If one tries to advance in this way, it will certainly lead to misfortune. Heed the warning.

2. *The gates to success begin to open.*
   Perseverence brings good fortune.

When resistance gives way, and we forge ahead, this is the point at which, only too easily, we become the prey of exuberant self-confidence. This is why perseverance in inner equilibrium, without excessive use of power, is so important. True power holds itself.

3. *The small man works through power;*
   But the wise man does not act this way.
   A goat that butts against a hedge
   Only gets its horns entangled.

Making a boast of power leads to entanglements. A small man will revel in power if it comes his way, but the wise man never makes this mistake. Mindful of the danger of pushing ahead, regardless, he renounces, in good time, the empty display of force.

4. *Persevere. Success comes: remorse goes.*
   The hedge opens: no entanglement.
   A big cart's power lies in its axle.

Through quiet perseverence, success comes in the end. Any remorse arising from the excessive use of power then disappears. A wise man's power does not show externally yet it can move heavy loads, like a big cart, whose real strength lies in its axle. The less that power is applied outwardly, the greater is its effect.

5. *One loses one's goat. Good. No regret.*

The goat is noted for its outer hardness and inner weakness. When things get easier and there is no more resistance, one can easily rid oneself of any obstinate disposition. Then can one give up a belligerent, stubborn way of acting and not have to regret it.

6. *A goat butts a hedge and gets entangled.*
   It can go neither forward nor backward.
   Take note: thus to overcome one's mistake.

If one goes too far, one comes to deadlock. One can neither advance nor retreat. Whatever one does only complicates things further. Such obstinacy leads to insuperable difficulties. But if one realises the situation and composes oneself, and desists, then everything will right itself in time. One must not stiffen in obstinacy, but yield.

35
EASY PROGRESS

≡≡ above   THE CLINGING, FIRE
     below   THE RECEPTIVE, EARTH

THE CONDITION
The image of the sun rising over the earth is the symbol of rapid, easy progress: ever-widening expansion and increasing clarity.

Three hexagrams mean progress: EASY PROGRESS, PUSHING UPWARD (46), symbolised by wood growing within the earth, and DEVELOPMENT (53), showing the still more gradual development of a tree on a mountain. All mean progress, but EASY PROGRESS is the finest of all.

THE JUDGMENT
A devoted prince brings others with him
To pledge fealty and peace to his king.
He is given honour, reward and influence.

The trigrams' attributes, clarity above and devotion below, represent, in human society, a wise ruler with devoted servitors.

A twofold idea is set forth:

The actual effect of progress emanates from a man who is in a dependent position and whom the others regard as their equal and are, therefore, willing to follow. This leader has enough clarity of vision not to abuse his great influence but, rather, to use it for the benefit of his ruler.

The ruler, in turn, free of all jealousy, showers presents on the great man and invites him continually to his court.

An enlightened ruler and an obedient servant: this is the condition upon which great progress depends. This is the way for the yielding to progress and gain influence.

THE IMAGE
As the sun rises over the earth,
Thus does the wise man brighten his virtue.
In 'Devotion to Great Clarity' is a path.

The light of the sun, as it rises over the earth, is, by nature, clear. The higher the sun rises, the more it emerges from the dark mists to spread its pure light over an ever-widening area. The real nature of man is, likewise, innately good. But it becomes clouded by contact with earthly things and so needs purification before it can shine forth with its innate clarity, its pristine purity.

In 'Devotion to Great Clarity' we have a model for a philosophy of life: what is innately light rises, of itself, over that which darkens: as the sun rises, of itself, unobstructed by the compliant earth.

DEGREES OF CHANGE

1. *Progressing but turned back. Persevere.*

Everything is pressing for progress, but one is still not sure of one's way. If one fears a rebuff, then simply continue to do what is right. In the end, this will bring favour. If one meets with no confidence, one should not try to win it, regardless of the situation, but remain calm and cheerful and refuse to be roused to anger. Thus one avoids mistakes.

2. *Progressing but frustrated. Persevere.*

When progress is halted because one is kept from getting in touch with the man in authority with whom one has an affinity, one must remain persevering, despite one's sorrow. In the end, great happiness will be bestowed; and be well-deserved, being based not on selfish or partisan motives, but on firm and correct principles.

3. *Progressing together. Remorse vanishes.*

When all are in accord, one can make progress with the backing and encouragement of others. Thus is dispelled any regret one may have: in that one lacks the independence to triumph, unaided, over every hostile turn of fate.

4. *Progressing like a rat brings danger.*

In times of progress it is easy for strong men, in the wrong places, to amass great wealth by stealth. Just as rats hide themselves by day, so also, such conduct shuns exposure. But times of progress are also times when dubious procedures are, inevitably, brought to light. Be warned. To persist in such action always leads to danger.

5. *Take not gain and loss to heart:*
   What matters is one's blessing.

When one finds oneself in an influential position, in a time of progress, one should remain gentle and reserved. One may reproach oneself for not having seized every possible advantage, but such regrets will pass away. Gain and loss are minor considerations: one is not dependent on external things. What matters much more is one's creation of opportunities for beneficent influence.

6. *Progress by force. Beware of dangers.*

Forceful progress is permissible only in dealing with the mistakes of one's own people. Even then, we must bear in mind its dangers, if we are to avoid mistakes. To persist too energetically, especially with those with whom we have no close connection, will lead to humiliation. Forceful progress is dangerous.

DARKENING OF THE LIGHT

≡≡ above THE RECEPTIVE, EARTH
≡≡ below THE CLINGING, FIRE

THE CONDITION

As the sun sinks below the earth, it is darkened. The light is 'wounded', injured. But it is only veiled, not extinguished.

In human terms, the situation is the opposite of EASY PROGRESS (35), where the sun rising over the earth symbolises a wise leader who has able helpers and, in company with them, makes progress.

Here, the sun sinking below the earth symbolises a time when a man of dark nature is in a position of authority, bringing harm to the wise and able man.

THE JUDGMENT

In adversity one must be persevering.
The light is veiled, not extinguished.
By clarity within and devotion without
One can overcome the greatest adversity.

One must not allow oneself to be swept along by unfavourable circumstances, nor permit one's steadfastness to be shaken.

One can avoid this by maintaining one's inner light whilst remaining outwardly yielding and tractable. In this way can one overcome even the greatest adversities.

In some situations, one must hide one's light in order to make one's will prevail in spite of difficulties in one's immediate environment. Perseverance must dwell in inmost consciousness and should not be outwardly discernible. Only thus can one remain steadfast in the face of adversity.

We are reminded (as in 9) of the example of good King Wên who, as a prince, was long held captive in the court of the tyrant Chou Hsin, with constant danger to his life.

THE IMAGE

As the light sinks into the earth,
So does the wise man live with the world:
He veils his light, yet still he shines.

In a time of darkness, it is essential to be cautious and reserved. One should not needlessly awaken overwhelming enmity by inconsiderate behaviour.

In such times one ought not to fall in with the practices of others; but nor should one drag them censoriously into the light.

In social intercourse one should not try to be all-knowing. One should let many things pass without being duped.

DEGREES OF CHANGE

1. *Flight and deprivation. But one has a goal.*
With grandiose resolve one tries to soar above all obstacles, but thus one encounters hostile fate, so one retreats and evades the issue. But if one does not want to make compromises with oneself, if one insists on remaining true to one's principles, then one suffers deprivation. Better to go hungry than eat without honour. Even one's friends misunderstand and speak ill of one. And yet, despite gossip, one still has one's goal.

2. *Though wounded, one can still give aid.*
Here, one's injury is not fatal but only a hindrance. Whilst rescue is still possible, the wounded man should give no thought to himself but think only of saving others also in danger. There is good fortune in acting thus: in accordance with one's duty.

3. *The dark one is captured. Avoid haste.*
As if by chance, the good man striving for order meets the ringleader of disorder and seizes him. Thus, the victory is won. But, in abolishing long-standing abuses, one must not be too hasty or harm will result.

4. *One gets to the heart of the darkness;*
But one must leave to save oneself.
One finds oneself close to the commander of darkness and so discovers his most secret thoughts. But nothing can be done. One must leave the scene of the disaster before the storm breaks. To stay on would mean sacrificing oneself to no purpose.

5. *If one cannot leave one's post,*
Persevere with redoubled caution.
If one cannot leave one's post, in times of darkness, one needs invincible perseverance of spirit and redoubled caution in one's dealings with the world. To escape danger one must conceal one's true sentiments and not allow external misery to deflect one from one's convictions.

6. *The dark power reaches its climax;*
But then perishes of its own darkness.
Evil must, of itself, fall at the very moment it has wholly overcome the good, for it has then consumed the energy to which it owed its duration. If one has the power to enlighten people but, instead, one makes it one's business to injure them, then one breaks the rule that binds one who governs. One thus prepares one's own downfall. As the sun rises, the sinister is unmasked: first, at the top.

37

THE FAMILY (THE CLAN)

☰ above   THE GENTLE, WIND
☲ below   THE CLINGING, FIRE

THE CONDITION

The symbol, wind created by fire, represents influence that goes out from within.

THE FAMILY shows the laws within the household that, transferred to outside life, keep society and the world in order.

THE FAMILY is society in embryo. It is the place where the performance of moral duty is made easy by natural affection.

Thus, within a small circle, a basis of moral practice is created which is then widened to include all human relations.

THE JUDGMENT

A good wife is persevering and loyal.

The foundation of the family is the relationship between husband and wife.

Within the family a strong authority is needed. This is vested in the parents. But the tie that holds the family together is the loyalty and perseverance of the wife.

Her place is within whilst that of the husband is without. It is in accord with the great laws of nature that husband and wife take their proper places.

In the family we see the three basic social relationships: between father and son, love; between husband and wife, chaste conduct; and, between two brothers, correctness.

When the family is in order, all mankind's social relationships will be in order: the reverence of a son reflects a prince's faithfulness to duty; the affection and correctness between two brothers reflects, firstly, loyalty to a friend and, secondly, deference to a person of superior rank.

THE IMAGE

As wind comes forth from fire,
So the wise man's words have substance,
For he has duration in his way of life.

As wind emanates from fire, so influence works from within outwards. In regulating the family, one's influence must proceed from one's own person. As flame depends on fuel so, to have power, one's words must be pertinent and based on reality, not general discourses which have no effect. Outgoing influence emanates from inner clarity.

One's words and one's conduct must accord and be consistent to have effect. If they do not accord, they will have no effect.

DEGREES OF CHANGE

1. *A child in firm seclusion. No regrets.*
Within the family unit, each must know his place. Each child must be accustomed to firmly established rules of order before ever its will is directed to other things. If we enforce order too late, the child is spoilt, for his will is already over-indulged. By insisting on order at the outset, remorse may arise; but it always disappears again and everything rights itself. Nothing is more easily avoided and more difficult to carry through than harnessing a child's will.

2. *The wife should not follow her whims.*
The wife should be guided by the will of the master of the house. Her great and important duties are within: to nourish her family and so become the centre of the social and spiritual life of the family. A good wife is devoted and gentle, seeking nothing by force. By her perseverance she brings favour to all.

3. *When tempers flare and one is too severe:*
   Remorse. But good fortune, none the less,
   For to dally all day ends in disgrace.
The proper mean between severity and indulgence should prevail. But, if in doubt, too great severity is preferable, because it preserves family discipline, whereas too great weakness leads to disgrace. It is wise for each individual to have complete freedom within clearly defined boundaries.

4. *The wife is the treasure of the house.*
Upon the wife, the family well-being depends. When income and expenditure are soundly balanced, good fortune results. This applies also in public life to a faithful steward whose measures further the general welfare.

5. *As a king, should he govern his family.*
A fatherly man, rich in wisdom, does nothing to make himself feared. He is trusted because love reigns. He does not achieve his ends by means of severity, but by love. His character, of itself, exercises the right influence.

6. *The master's work commands respect.*
In the final analysis, order within the family depends on the character of the master of the house. He should cultivate his personality so that it works through the force of inner truth. He makes demands, first of all, upon himself. Such strength and stability brings favour for all. If one is in this ruling position one must, of one's own accord, assume its responsibilities.

38

OPPOSITION

☰	above	THE CLINGING, FIRE
☱	below	THE JOYOUS, LAKE

THE CONDITION

Fire and water are, by nature, opposed. Fire burns upwards; water seeps downwards. These two movements are opposed, hence the idea of opposition, estrangement, misunderstanding: of wills divergently directed.

When people live in opposition and estrangement they cannot carry out great undertakings in common because their points of view diverge too widely.

THE JUDGMENT

Opposition in small matters leads to union
And thence to good fortune.
Great indeed is the effect
Of the time of opposition.

In times of opposition, one should not proceed brusquely, for that would only increase the existing opposition. Instead, one should limit oneself to producing gradual effects in small matters.

When opposition does not preclude all agreement, success can be expected.

In general, opposition appears as an obstruction. But when it represents polarity within a comprehensive whole, it has its useful and important functions.

The oppositions of heaven and earth, of spirit and nature, of man and woman, when reconciled, bring about the creation and reproduction of life.

In the world of visible things, it is the principle of opposites that makes possible the differentiation by categories through which order is brought into the world.

The trigrams' attributes show the way of reconciliation. Joyousness (within) unites, whilst clarity (without) finds the right way.

Opposition creates the need for a bridge. Thus is opposition the natural prerequisite of union: it is a phase to be transcended.

THE IMAGE

As fire and water never commingle
And, even in contact, retain their natures;
So, amid all fellowship,
The wise man retains his individuality.

The wise man is never led into baseness or vulgarity through contact or community of interest with persons of another sort.

Regardless of all commingling, he will always preserve his individuality.

DEGREES OF CHANGE

1. *If you lose your horse, do not chase it:*
   It will come back of its own accord.
   If you see evil people, avoid mistakes.

A horse goes further and further away if one runs after it. Likewise, if someone who belongs with us is temporarily estranged, due to a misunderstanding, he will come back of his own accord if we leave matters to him.

On the other hand, if evil men, who do not belong with us, force themselves upon us, it is important to avoid mistakes. To try to shake them off by force would give rise to real hostility. We must endure them.

2. *One meets his lord in a narrow street.*

An accidental meeting under informal circumstances may serve to bring together people estranged by a misunderstanding, providing they have an inner affinity. No blame if one meets this way. One has not lost one's way.

3. *One sees oneself hindered and insulted.*
   Not a good beginning, but a good end.

It often seems to one that everything is conspiring against one. One must not let oneself be misled. Despite opposition, one must cleave to that with which one knows one belongs. Thus will the matter end well.

4. *Isolated through opposition. Danger.*
   But one meets a like-minded companion.
   Association in good faith. No blame.

By inner opposition to those around one, one becomes isolated. But if one meets a man with whom one has an inner affinity, and whom one can trust completely, one overcomes the dangers of isolation. Thus can one succeed.

5. *A companion overcomes the estrangement.*
   One should go with him and find blessing.

One may fail, at first, to recognise a sincere man at times of general estrangement. But, when such a man does reveal his true character, it is one's duty to meet with him and to work with him. It is the man of higher rank that must go to meet the other, for a man of ability will not come to offer himself.

6. *One sees one's friends as sly. Danger.*
   But then tension goes and union comes.

One misjudges even one's best friends due to inner isolation and estrangement. One becomes defensive. But, if one realises one's mistake and their best intentions, then the tension will be resolved in union and all will go well. Just when opposition reaches its climax, it changes over to its antithesis.

39
OBSTRUCTION

☵ **above** THE ABYSMAL, WATER
☶ **below** KEEPING STILL, MOUNTAIN

THE CONDITION

The hexagram pictures a dangerous abyss lying before us and a steep, inaccessible mountain rising behind us.

We are surrounded by obstacles.

But the mountain, whose attribute is keeping still, provides a hint as to how we can extricate ourselves. In the face of danger without, we must keep still within.

It is by turning inward that our attention is directed to overcoming obstacles.

Obstruction is not a lasting condition.

THE JUDGMENT

> *To see danger and know how to stand still:*
> *That is wisdom.*
> *One should pause and seek wise counsel.*

One is confronted by obstacles that cannot be overcome directly. Obstructions are not overcome by pressing forward into danger, nor by idly keeping still, but by retreating, yielding. But one retreats only to prepare for overcoming the obstruction.

One should join forces with like-minded friends and put oneself under the leadership of a man who is equal to the situation.

Just when one must do something that seems to lead away from one's goal, one needs the will to persevere. It is such unswerving inner purpose that brings good fortune in the end.

An obstruction that lasts only for a time is useful for self-development. This is the value of adversity. An inferior man will bewail his fate and seek to put the blame on others. A wise man will seek the error within himself. In this way external obstacles become, for him, occasions for inner enrichment and education.

THE IMAGE

> *Water on a mountain: progress obstructed.*
> *Thus a wise man turns inward to himself;*
> *Thus does he mould his character.*

Water on the top of a mountain cannot flow down because it is obstructed: rocks hinder it. It must stand still. Then does it increase until the inner accumulation finally becomes so great that it overflows the barriers.

The way of overcoming obstacles lies in turning inward and raising one's own being to a higher level. Obstructions and difficulties throw a wise man back upon himself.

DEGREES OF CHANGE

1. *When going ahead leads to obstructions,*
   One should retreat and wait.

When one encounters an obstruction, it is important to reflect on how best to deal with it. When danger threatens, to strive blindly ahead leads to complications. The correct way is to retreat: not in order to give up the struggle, but to await the right moment for action.

2. *A king's servant, beset by obstructions.*
   If one's path of duty leads to danger,
   Then one must confront it. No blame.

Normally it is best to go around obstacles, but if a man's duty, in the service of a higher cause, is to seek out danger and to confront it, he may do so without compunction, even though difficulty piles upon difficulty. It is not through any fault of his that he puts himself into danger. No blame.

3. *A father is obstructed, so he comes back.*

Unlike the king's servant, compelled by duty to follow the way of danger, a father has a duty to his family. If he were to plunge recklessly into danger, it would be a useless act because those entrusted to his care cannot get along by themselves. He should retreat. His kin will welcome him with joy.

4. *When going leads to obstructions,*
   Coming back leads to union with friends.

The situation cannot be managed single-handedly. If one presses ahead alone, on one's own strength, unprepared, one miscalculates and fails to find support. Better, therefore, to retreat and gather trustworthy companions who can be counted upon to help in overcoming the obstructions.

5. *The greatest obstructions bring help.*

If one is called to help, in an emergency, one should not seek to evade the obstacle, however dangerous. If one is really called to the task, one's spirit will be so strong as to attract helpers whom one can organise so that the obstruction is overcome.

6. *It furthers one to see the great man.*

This refers to a sage who has withdrawn from the world and its tumult. In adverse times he may be tempted to turn his back on the world and to abandon it. But this way is barred to him. Duty calls him back, once more, into the turmoil of life. It is because of his experience and inner freedom that he can create great things and bring favour to all.

40

DELIVERANCE

above   THE AROUSING, THUNDER

below   THE ABYSMAL, WATER

THE CONDITION

DELIVERANCE is movement that goes out of the sphere of danger. The upper trigram, THE AROUSING, denotes movement up and away from the lower trigram, THE ABYSMAL, danger. Hence the idea of release, deliverance.

But the deliverance is not yet achieved. It is just in its beginning and the six DEGREES OF CHANGE represent its stages.

The image is a thunderstorm. When a thunderstorm breaks, the whole of nature breathes freely again, tension is released, and heaven and earth deliver themselves.

The time of DELIVERANCE is great indeed.

THE JUDGMENT

At the time of DELIVERANCE
One should seek to return to the regular.
If there are things to be done,
One should attend to them quickly.

When tensions and complications begin to be eased, we should make our way back to ordinary conditions as soon as we can.

Such periods of sudden change are of great importance. Just as thunder and rain relieve atmospheric tension, making all the buds burst open, so too, deliverance from burdensome pressure has a liberating and stimulating effect on life.

But it is important, in such times, not to overdo our triumph or push on further than is necessary. Returning to the regular order of life as soon as deliverance is achieved is the way that leads to good fortune.

If there are any residual matters that ought to be attended to, then see to them as quickly as possible so that a clean sweep is made and no retardations occur.

THE IMAGE

As thunder and rain deliver nature,
So does the wise man pardon and forgive.

As a thunderstorm clears the air, so the wise man produces like effects in dealing with the mistakes and sins of men: the original cause of conditions of tension.

The failings of men (the unintentional transgressions) he does not dwell upon; their mistakes he passes over as thunder dies away. Even wilful sins he forgives, as water washes all things clean.

By his clarity does he bring deliverance.

DEGREES OF CHANGE

1. *When deliverance has come,*
   Take rest, keep still and use few words.

When the hindrance is past and deliverance has come, then is the time to keep still and to recuperate in peace. In this way is order brought into the situation.

2. *He catches cunning foxes in the field*
   And receives a yellow arrow as reward.
   By perseverance comes inner strength.

The obstacles in public life are like designing foxes who try to influence the ruler by flattery. Only by their removal can deliverance come. But one's weapons must be correct. Yellow is the colour of moderation and mean in proceeding against the enemy: the arrow signifies the straight course, rectitude. By whole-hearted devotion to the task of deliverance, one gains such inner strength and rectitude that one is armed against all that is false and low.

3. *A peasant rides in a golden carriage.*
   To persist this way leads to disgrace.

If a man is delivered out of need into comfort and freedom from want but, like an upstart, he tries to take his ease in a sumptuous style unsuited to his nature, he flaunts himself and attracts robbers. Are not sumptuous ornaments worn by a maiden enticements to rob her of her virtue?

4. *Deliver yourself from inferior people.*
   Only then can come trustworthy friends.

In times of standstill, inferior people attach themselves to wise men and even grow close by force of habit. But when deliverance comes, with its call to deeds, one must free oneself of such chance acquaintances, otherwise reliable, like-minded friends will mistrust one and stay away.

5. *The wise man must deliver himself*
   And so prove, to the small, his resolve.

Times of deliverance demand inner resolve. Inferior people will not be put off by external means. One must break with them completely, in one's mind, so they will see that one is in earnest and withdraw.

6. *A wise man bides his time, then acts.*
   Deliverance by force is a last resort.

When wickedness in high places is so hardened that it can withstand even the force of inner influence, external force becomes necessary. But only a man of authority can act this way; and then, only when he is sure.

41

DECREASE

≡≡ above   KEEPING STILL, MOUNTAIN

≡≡ below   THE JOYOUS, LAKE

THE CONDITION

In DECREASE the lower trigram has, as it were, lost a strong, light line in favour of the upper trigram. When what is below is decreased to the benefit of what is above, this is out-and-out decrease.

If the foundations of a building are decreased to add strength to the upper walls, the whole structure loses its stability.

In human terms, decrease in the prosperity of the people in favour of the government is out-and-out decrease.

THE JUDGMENT

> *At a time of decrease,*
> *Sincerity brings great good fortune. No blame.*
> *For God accepts the simplest sacrifice.*

Whilst INCREASE, through fullness, ushers in decline, when DECREASE has reached its goal, flowering is sure to begin.

Decrease is not always bad. Decrease and increase come in their own time. One must understand and go with the time and not try to cover poverty with empty pretence.

In such a time, thrift is no disgrace.

If a time of scanty resources brings out inner truth; one must not be ashamed of simplicity; for simplicity is then the very thing needed to provide the inner strength for further undertakings.

Do not be concerned if the outer beauty of one's culture, or even the elaboration of religious forms, have to suffer because of simplicity. Inner strength compensates for what is lacking in externals. The power of content makes up for simplicity of form.

There is no need of presenting false appearances to God. Even with slender means true sentiment can be expressed.

THE IMAGE

> *As a lake below enriches a mountain above;*
> *As decrease below gives increase above;*
> *Thus does the wise man curb his passions.*

Joy can develop into unchecked gaiety: passionate drives that expend life forces. Stubborn strength (the mountain) can harden into anger. So decrease is doubly necessary.

To cultivate one's character one must decrease anger by keeping still; decrease passion by restriction. Thus is one's lower nature decreased and the higher enriched.

DEGREES OF CHANGE

1. *Self-decrease to serve others is good.*
   But how much may one decrease others?

It is good for one to use one's strength in the service of others: helping quickly where needed, neither bragging nor making much of it.

If one is in receipt of such aid, one must weigh carefully how much one can accept without one's helper being soured. Avoid inconsiderate demands.

Likewise, only where such delicacy of feeling exists can one give oneself unconditionally, without hesitation.

2. *Increasing others*
   Without decreasing oneself.

If one throws oneself away at the bidding of a superior, one decreases oneself but gives no lasting benefit to the other. This is wrong. The correct mean, based on true self-awareness, is to serve without demeaning oneself. No forfeit of dignity is necessary for one to serve others.

3. *Increase and decrease: both give measure.*
   Two is company; three is too many;
   And one man alone needs a companion.

The excessive must be decreased and the insufficient increased to give true measure. A very close bond is possible only between two people. When there are three, jealousy and mistrust arise: they must decrease by one. But one man alone needs a companion to complement him: as heaven and earth, male and female, Yang and Yin, complement each other. By such union are all beings created.

4. *By decreasing one's faults and one's self*
   One increases one's circle. No mistake.

One's faults, sometimes reinforced by one's environment, often prevent well-disposed people from drawing closer. Seek humility. By bringing oneself to give them up one frees such friends from inner pressure so they may approach one, bringing mutual joy.

5. *One is increased, indeed, by blessing.*

When fate favours one, as if ordained from on high, one need fear nothing. If one is favoured by fate then favour will surely come.

6. *If one is increased, no blame. Persevere.*
   Seek not private gain, but helpers.

There are some people who bring blessing to the whole world. Their increase benefits all and so decreases no one. But only by hard work and perseverance can success be won and helpers found as needed. What is gained in this way benefits and increases all people.

42

INCREASE

above   THE GENTLE, WIND
below   THE AROUSING, THUNDER

THE CONDITION
The idea of increase is expressed in the lower trigram being given a strong line from the upper trigram. When what is above sacrifices itself to increase what is below, this is out-and-out increase.

As heaven dispenses and earth brings forth: in this way are all things increased.

True increase is without artifice.

The sacrifice, self-abnegation, of the higher element produces out-and-out increase in the lower element.

Herein is expressed the most basic principle of leadership: to rule truly is to serve.

It is this spirit alone that has power to help the world. It is the way of great enlightenment; the way of great clarity.

THE JUDGMENT
As the moon waxes, but then wanes;
As do the seasons come and go;
So the time of increase does not endure.
We should utilise it, whilst it lasts,
To undertake something great.

Sacrifice on the part of those above for the increase of those below fills people with a sense of joy and gratitude which is of great value to the common well-being.

When people are thus devoted to their leaders, great and difficult undertakings are possible. Therefore, in such times of progress and successful development, it is necessary to work and make the best use of the time, in harmony with its spirit.

THE IMAGE
As thunder and wind reinforce each other,
So the wise man notes the ways of others.
If he sees good in others, he imitates it;
If he sees bad in himself, he removes it.

Whilst observing how thunder and wind increase and strengthen each other, a wise man notes the way of self-increase and self-improvement. When he discovers good in others, he imitates it and thus makes everything good on earth his own. If he perceives something bad in himself, he rids himself of it, as the wind breaks up and dissolves shadowy and dark clouds:

In this way does one become free of evil. This moral change represents the most important increase of one's personality.

DEGREES OF CHANGE

1. *One should undertake something great.*
   Good fortune comes from selflessness.

If grace and favour come to one from on high, one should use one's increased strength to achieve something great: some great deed for which one would otherwise have neither the energy to undertake, nor the readiness to take responsibility for. Good fortune comes from selflessness. Go this way. No blame.

2. *Love of the good brings real increase.*

One brings about real increase by cultivating in oneself the right conditions: receptivity and love of the good. Then, what one strives for will come, of itself, with the inevitability of natural law. Where increase is in harmony with the highest laws of the universe, nothing can stop it. But one must be steadfast, lest unexpected good fortune make one heedless. Make it one's own through inner strength. Then can one stand, before God and man, and accomplish something for the good of the world.

3. *One is enriched, even by misfortune,*
   If one is sincere and correct.

At times of blessing and enrichment, even events ordinarily unfortunate turn out to be of advantage. By becoming free of error and by acting in harmony with the truth, one gains such inner authority that one exerts influence as if sanctioned from above.

4. *He who reports to the prince*
   Must walk in the middle.

An official who mediates between leaders and followers must be disinterested. Such a man not only spreads benefits from the leader to the people, holding nothing back in a selfish way, but he also exercises a good influence on the leader. Such a man is especially important at times of increase and great undertakings. Such a man shapes the future for he has the inner assent of all.

5. *True kindness does not seek honours:*
   It acts from inner necessity.

The truly kind heart is rewarded not in being honoured but in being recognised. Then can the benficent influence spread unhindered.

6. *He, who increases no one, brings misfortune.*

If one is obdurate, aloof, one-sided, and not concerned to increase others, one will soon lose influence and invite attack. Brusquerie kills co-operation; agitated words awaken no echo in others. The wise man composes his mind before he speaks. His way is his security.

43

BREAK-THROUGH (RESOLUTENESS)

≡≡ **above** THE JOYOUS, LAKE
below THE CREATIVE, HEAVEN

THE CONDITION

The hexagram signifies a break-through after a long accumulation of tension.

When strength has accumulated within a lake it breaks through its dykes. When a lake has evaporated to heaven, it breaks through in the manner of a cloudburst.

In human terms, the single dark line in the outermost place in the hexagram refers to a time when inferior people begin to disappear and their influence is on the wane.

In BREAK-THROUGH it is as a result of resolute action that conditions are changed.

THE JUDGMENT

> *By resolution is evil overcome:*
> *In high places, denounced despite danger;*
> *In oneself, not by force but by the good.*

Just one inferior man in a ruling position is able to oppress superior men. Just one single passion lurking in the heart has the power to obscure reason.

Passion and reason cannot co-exist. One must fight without quarter if the good is to prevail. But in the struggle of good against evil there are four rules we cannot disregard:

* When strength sees weakness above it, there is danger of defiance. Resolution must be based on a union of strength and goodwill.
* Compromise with evil is not possible. It must be honestly discredited: not least in one's own passions and shortcomings.
* Direct force must not be used for it leads to entanglement in hatred and passion, and thus, we lose in the end. As long as we fight evil, blow for blow, it will prevail.
* Finally, the best way to fight evil is to make energetic progress in the good.

THE IMAGE

> *As water rises to heaven to give rain;*
> *So the wise man dispenses his riches.*

A lake accumulated in heaven gives reason to fear a cloudburst. To pile up riches for oneself alone leads surely to a collapse.

All gathering is followed by dispersion, so the wise man distributes as he gathers.

So also, in developing his character, he takes care to avoid resolution hardening into obstinacy. He remains open to impressions and avoids pride and self-satisfaction by the help of strict and continuous self-examination.

DEGREES OF CHANGE

1. *To over-reach oneself is a mistake.*

In resolute advance, new beginnings are especially difficult. We feel inspired to press forward but resistance is still strong. We must gauge our own strength and venture only so far as we can with the certainty of success. To plunge blindly ahead is wrong. It is precisely at the beginning that unexpected setbacks can be most disastrous.

2. *Despite danger and alarm, fear nothing,*
   For one is forearmed with caution.

Readiness is everything. Resolution must be bound up with caution. If one is careful, even before danger comes, one is forearmed. Be alert to what is not yet in sight, and one need fear nothing. As reason triumphs, the passions withdraw of themselves. To be circumspect and not to forget one's armour is the right way to security.

3. *Despite censure and gossip, be resolved.*
   Remain true to yourself. No blame.

A difficult situation. In the resolute fight against the inferior, one often cannot cut one's relationship with an inferior man too quickly, or he would take countermeasures and so endanger the entire situation. Even though one is alone and misunderstood, one must endure this and remain true to oneself. Only when the time is ripe should one turn against the inferior. Time will show one's way is true.

4. *Inner obstinacy. Good counsel ignored.*

He who wants to push forward under any circumstances, regardless of insuperable obstacles, is obstinate. If only he would desist, all would go well. But he ignores even this advice. Obstinacy makes a man unable to hear, even though he has ears.

5. *Dealing with weeds requires resolution.*

Weeds always grow back again and are difficult to eradicate. In the struggle against the inferior, there is always the danger that one may give up the battle as hopeless. Do not be deflected. Be resolute. By walking in the middle can one stay free of blame.

6. *A seeming victory. But then misfortune.*

Just when victory is won and everything seems easy, there is danger. If we are not on guard evil will succeed in escaping by stealth and grow again. Evil does not die easily. To deal with evil in ourselves we must be thorough. If we are careless, if we overlook anything, new evil will arise again from its seeds.

44

ENCOUNTERING (COMING TO MEET)

≡ above THE CREATIVE, HEAVEN

≡ below THE GENTLE, WIND

THE CONDITION
The hexagram represents a situation where the dark principle (the Yin line), after having been eliminated, furtively and unexpectedly re-enters from within and below.

Of its own accord the dark principle has come to meet the light principle as when, after the summer solstice, the dark principle begins to become ascendant again. The situation is unfavourable and dangerous. We must understand it and promptly prevent the possible consequences.

THE JUDGMENT
The way of inferior men increases
Because superior men lend them power.

When a bold girl lightly surrenders herself and gains power, she succeeds only because the superior element co-operates and meets the inferior element half-way. One should not marry such a maiden.

When an inferior thing seems so harmless that a man imagines he may dally with it and come to no harm, he gives it power.

Inferior men rise only because superior men do not regard them as dangerous and so lend them power. The inferior man always has to depend on a lucky chance.

If the inferior is resisted from the first, it can never gain influence.

But COMING TO MEET is also important in another way; a beneficial way.

Although, as a general rule, the weak should not come to meet the strong, there are times when this has great significance.

When earth comes to meet heaven, all creatures come into being and prosper.

When a prince and his official come to meet, the world is put in order.

When elements, destined to come together, meet each other half-way, their meeting must be free of dishonest or ulterior motives; otherwise, harm will result.

THE IMAGE
As the wind encounters all under heaven,
So the wise ruler spreads his commands.

As heaven is far from the things of the earth, but sets them in motion by means of the wind, so the wise ruler, though far from his people, sets them in motion by means of his commands and decrees. That is his work.

DEGREES OF CHANGE

1. *Even a lean pig has it in him to rage.*
A lean pig is weak but, after it has eaten its fill and become strong, its true nature will come out, if not previously curbed. If an inferior element has wormed its way in, it must be checked at once, By consistent checking can one prevent the bad effects of letting such things take their course. Let not the insignificance of that which creeps in tempt one to underrate it. It is right that the weak should be led.

2. *In penning the pig; be gentle; be firm.*
Inferior elements are not overcome by violence but by means of gentle control. To a pig, a pen is not a prison but a home. By such control one need not fear evil. But beware, lest it get free to rage about unchecked and spread its evil influence.

3. *Temptation and painful indecision.*
   Aware of danger, one avoids big mistakes.
One may be tempted to fall in with the evil element offering itself but, here, circumstances prevent this: one would like to, but cannot. By gaining a clear insight into the dangers one avoids big mistakes.

4. *Aloof because ambitious. Misfortune.*
An official who neglects to keep in touch with the people because he strives upward has the wrong inner attitude. It is our own fault if we become alienated from less important people and do not meet them half-way. They will turn their backs on us and not be available when we need them.

5. *As a ripe fruit falls from heaven,*
   So others fall to one's disposition.
Fate is kind to the right leader. A strong, wise, well-poised man will tolerate and protect those in his charge. He will not try to impress them with outward show, or rely on tiresome admonitions, but put his trust in the transforming effect of a strong and upright personality. They will then fall to his disposition like ripe fruit: fruit that ripens of its own accord.

6. *If the high and proud wish to be so*
   Then one should let them be.
Men often find the world and its tumult unbearable, so they withdraw from it and hold themselves aloof. If they encounter anything lowly they rebuff it brusquely. What does it matter if they are disliked? They know how to bear it with composure.

45

GATHERING TOGETHER

above   THE JOYOUS, LAKE

below   THE RECEPTIVE, EARTH

THE CONDITION

A lake is a place where waters gather.

People gather together for natural reasons, as do members of a family, or for artificial ones, as in the case of a state.

The trigrams' attributes, devotion within and joyousness without, show the basis of gathering together among men.

THE JUDGMENT

When the king approaches his temple,
One should come too, with one's offering,
For this is the time for great undertakings.

When the family gathers about the father as its head, the family ancestors are honoured and, through the collective piety of the living members, become so integrated in the spiritual life of the family that it cannot be dispersed or dissolved.

Where men gather together, religious forces are needed. But there must also be a human leader to serve as the centre of the group.

If he would bring others together, a leader must, first of all, be collected within himself.

The religious significance of gathering together is expressed in great offerings.

The secular significance of gathering together is expressed in great deeds.

When great deeds are favoured by the time then, to undertake something great, is devotion to the command of heaven. Such great times of unification will always leave great achievements behind them.

As heaven is the bond of union in nature, so ancestors are the bond of union among men. If one knows these forces, all relationships become clear. Only collective moral force can unite the world: the union of devotion and joy.

THE IMAGE

As a lake gathers the waters on earth,
So also, men come to gather together.
Then does the wise man renew his weapons,
In order to meet the unforeseen.

As a lake may gather until it overflows, so, there is danger in gathering together, and precautions must be taken. Where men gather in great numbers, strife may come: where possessions are gathered, robbery may occur.

We must arm promptly against the unexpected for in this way come human woes. If we are prepared, forearmed, they can be prevented.

90

DEGREES OF CHANGE

1. *Without a leader, wills grow confused:*
   But one who can lead brings laughter.

When men desire to gather around a leader they can look up to, but there is none, they become confused and waver in their decision. But, if they express their need and call for help, then just one grasp of the hand from the leader is enough to turn away all distress and restore joy. Nevertheless, a group must never allow itself to be led astray.

2. *Letting oneself be drawn by affinity:*
   Even one's small offering is acceptable.

One should not choose one's way arbitrarily but yield to the influence of hidden inner forces that bring together those who belong together. Where inner bonds exist, no great preparations or formalities are necessary. People understand and accept one another just as God accepts even a small offering if it comes from the heart. Therefore, be sincere.

3. *If one is an outsider, seek alliance:*
   In spite of humiliation this way is right.

If one wishes to unite with others but they have already formed a group, one feels isolated. One must then choose one's way. To ally oneself with someone who can help one to gain admission to the group is, despite any initial humiliation, no mistake.

4. *A minister who gathers men around him,*
   In the name of his ruler, brings favour.

A minister must not strive for any special advantage for himself, but work unselfishly to bring about general unity. By claiming no merit for himself does his work develop correctly – to be crowned with success.

5. *A leader gains sway. No blame in this.*
   But he must also win the insincere.

When people gather around a man, not out of confidence in him but merely because of his influential position, he must gain their confidence by steadfast, intensified and unswerving devotion to duty. As his will grows clearer, so secret mistrust is overcome and any remorse will disappear.

6. *Lamenting and sighing, floods of tears:*
   This is the right way. It may succeed.

If one wishes to ally oneself with another, but one's intentions are misunderstood, one laments. No blame: for this may well cause the other to come to his senses so that the alliance one seeks, and so painfully misses, can be achieved, after all.

46
PUSHING UPWARD

☷ above   THE RECEPTIVE, EARTH

☴ below   THE GENTLE, WOOD

THE CONDITION

The picture of wood growing within the earth gives the idea of PUSHING UPWARD.

In contrast to EASY PROGRESS (35), where the sun rising over the earth indicates easy expansion, PUSHING UPWARD is associated with effort, as a plant, needing energy for pushing upward.

What is indicated here is a vertical ascent by force of will, yet in harmony with the time, from obscurity and lowliness to power and influence.

Pushing upward begins at the bottom.

That which pushes upward does not come back.

THE JUDGMENT

PUSHING UPWARD has supreme success.
One should see great men: seek advice:
And set to work; for activity is favoured.

When the pushing upward of good elements encounters no obstruction it succeeds.

The gentle is within; devotion is without. Pushing upward is made possible not by violence, but by modesty and adaptability.

Borne along by the propitiousness of the time: thus does one make advance.

One need not fear seeing authoritative people, for success is assured by the time.

The reason for success is not an earthly but transcendental one. The favourableness of conditions comes from the invisible world.

We should make the most of the time, whilst we can, through work.

THE IMAGE

As wood grows within the earth,
So the wise man, of devoted character,
Heaps up small things
To achieve something high and great.

Like the gradual, invisible growth of wood within the earth, so the wise man makes steady, imperceptible progress.

As wood grows within the earth, without haste, without rest, so does the wise man never pause in his progress.

As wood bends round obstacles as it grows, so he adapts himself to conditions. Gentle and devoted, he pushes upward with the time.

To understand how a tree is contracted into a seed is to understand the future unfolding of the seed into a tree. To know this movement is to know the future.

DEGREES OF CHANGE

1. *Pushing upward meets with confidence.*
   Thus can something be accomplished.

At the beginning of ascent it is spiritual affinity, solidarity with that which is above, that creates the confidence needed to accomplish something. Just as wood draws strength for its upward push from the root, in itself, the lowliest place, so the power to rise comes from lowliness and obscurity. Growth arises from innate humility.

2. *If one is sincere and upright*
   One should bring even a small offering.

Even though a strong man may be somewhat brusque and pay too little attention to form, he can still meet with response from above if he is sincere. Where spiritual affinity is close, even small gifts do not harm mutual confidence. Uprightness comes from within. Correct growth requires uprightness.

3. *Easy, unobstructed progress.*

When things proceed with remarkable ease, one should profit from the propitiousness of the time. It is not wise to question one's luck, or to yield to misgivings, because they only inhibit one. But, equally, one must never rely upon future good fortune.

4. *The king offers one great honour.*
   This is the way of the devoted.

When pushing upward attains its goal, one acquires greatness, honour and fame. One is received into the circle of those who foster the spiritual life of the nation. In this way does one's significance endure beyond time.

5. *Pushing upward by steps. Persevere.*

When advancing, it is important not to become intoxicated by success. Precisely at the moment of success, it is necessary to remain sober and not try to skip any stages. Go slowly, step by step, as if hesitant. Only calm, steady progress leads to the goal. Just when one's will is achieved, is the time when perseverance is of great importance.

6. *Pushing upward in darkness. Exhaustion.*
   One must persevere unremittingly.

He who pushes upward blindly deludes himself. He knows only advance, not retreat, so he becomes exhausted. When things are unclear one must hold fast to the steadfastness which lies below consciousness, if one is not to lose one's way. Be conscientious and consistent and remain so. Thus does one avoid blind impulse which is always harmful.

47

OPPRESSION (EXHAUSTION)

above   THE JOYOUS, LAKE

below   THE ABYSMAL, WATER

THE CONDITION

The hexagram pictures a lake that is empty. It is dried up, exhausted, because an abyss has opened up within it and beneath it.

When there is no water in the lake, conditions are exceptional.

It represents a time of adversity when, everywhere, superior men are oppressed and held in restraint by inferior men.

OPPRESSION means encountering adverse fate. It is something that happens by chance.

THE JUDGMENT

OPPRESSION is a test of character:
It leads to perplexity and thence to success.
When one has something to say
One gets no hearing; one is not believed.
But through oppression does one learn
To lessen one's rancour.

Although they are the opposite of times of success, times of adversity can lead to success if they befall the right man.

When a strong man meets with adversity, he remains cheerful, despite all danger. This cheerfulness is the source of later successes for it comes of a stability of character that is stronger than fate.

But he who lets his spirit be broken by exhaustion certainly has no success.

If adversity only bends a man, it creates in him a power to react that is bound to manifest itself in due course.

No inferior man is capable of this.

Only a great man can bring about good fortune by keeping blameless and correct.

When outward influence is denied to one, because one's words have no effect, one must be strong within and sparing of words.

He who considers the mouth important falls into perplexity.

THE IMAGE

The lake is dried up, exhausted.
When adverse fate befalls him,
The wise man stakes his life
On following his will. .

At times of adverse fate there is nothing one can do but to acquiesce in one's fate and remain true to oneself.

This concerns the deepest stratum of one's being, for this alone is superior to all external fate.

DEGREES OF CHANGE

1. *One sits oppressed under a bare tree:*
   One strays into a gloomy valley.

When adversity befalls one, it is important, above all, to be strong and to overcome the trouble inwardly. If one is weak, trouble overwhelms one. If, instead of proceeding on one's way, one sits under a bare tree, one falls ever more deeply into gloom and melancholy. Such an attitude only makes the situation more and more hopeless. It is inner delusion that must be overcome.

2. *Oppressed whilst at meat and drink.*

One has the necessities of life, but one is exhausted by its commonplaces. This is inner oppression. One should seek to overcome obstructions in the inner world by offerings and prayer: inner preparation for later activity. To set forth without preparation would be most foolhardy. One must overcome inner oppression by patience of spirit.

3. *One feels oppresssed by walls of stone:*
   One leans on thorns and thistles.

Adverse times make one restless and indecisive. One wants to push ahead, but meets with obstructions that, at other times, one could easily overcome but, at this time, oppress one. It is one's approach that is wrong. One butts one's head against a wall and then feels oppressed by the wall. One leans on things that lack stability: they give one no rest. Irresolution brings no one rest.

4. *Oppressed whilst in a golden carriage.*

If a richer man sees need and seeks to help others less fortunate than himself, but finds that he cannot withdraw from his circle of wealthy and powerful friends, he hesitates. But his embarrassment will pass. His strength of will will bring him back to his goal.

5. *Oppressed with good intentions.*

If a man of goodwill finds no helpers, even among those whom he would expect to help in helping others, he must be patient. Things will improve. Meanwhile, he should pray for the general well-being, be firm in inner composure, and contemplate the divine.

6. *Oppressed by bonds one now can break.*

As one's distress draws to an end, one can easily master the oppression with insight. If one is still irresolute and influenced by one's previous condition, one fears to make a move. One must now grasp the situation, change one's attitude and be decisive.

48

THE WELL

≡≡
≡≡
≡≡

above THE ABYSMAL, WATER

below THE GENTLE, WOOD

THE CONDITION

The image derives from the pole-and-bucket well of ancient China: wood goes down into water in order to bring it up.

Likewise, in nature, the roots of plants go down to lift water out of the earth.

THE WELL is seen as an inexhaustible source of nourishment; the springs of life.

In political terms, THE WELL represents the abiding, unchanging nature of man's deepest needs. It represents the centre of the social structure and of social life.

THE JUDGMENT

The town may change but the well abides.
But if one's rope is too short,
Or if one breaks the jug,
Then one's thirst remains. Misfortune.

THE WELL is the unchanging within change. Capital cities may change as dynasties come and go but the well abides.

The well meets man's most basic needs. It is independent of all political forms.

As generations come and go, the life force goes on, inexhaustibly, for one and all.

Time and place may change but the ways of regulating social life remain the same.

However, there are two prerequisites for the satisfactory political or social organisation of mankind:
* We must go down to the very foundations of life. Any merely superficial ordering of life leaves deepest needs unsatisfied. It is as ineffectual as doing nothing.
* Carelessness is also disastrous. If, for example, military defence is carried to excess it actually provokes unrest and self-defeat.

THE WELL also applies to individuals. However men may differ in rank or learning, their basic human nature is the same. All can draw from the well-spring of the divine within human nature: but it requires deep penetration to its roots. One must be neither shallow nor careless in self-development.

THE IMAGE

As a plant lifts water to lift itself,
So a wise ruler encourages his people
To work and to help one another.

A wise man organises human society so that, like a plant, all its parts co-operate for the benefit of the whole.

DEGREES OF CHANGE

1. *No one drinks the mud of the well:*
   No animals come to an old well:
   Time just passes it by.

If one wanders in swampy lowlands, one's life is muddied. One loses all significance. One is outside life's movement. He who throws himself away is not sought out by others. In the end, no one bothers.

2. *The water is clear, but one's jug leaks:*
   One has left one's well to the fishes.

One has good qualities but neglects them. So, no one bothers. One deteriorates in mind and associates with inferior people. One can no longer achieve anything worthwhile. One's well is not used. No one comes to draw its water, however clear.

3. *The well is clear but no one drinks.*
   If only the king were clear-minded,
   Good fortune could be enjoyed by all.

An able man is available but no use is made of him. This sorrows those who know him. One wishes that the ruler might learn about it so that everyone might benefit.

4. *The well is being lined. No blame;*
   Because it is being put in order.

If a well is being reconditioned, lined with stone, it cannot be used whilst the work is going on. The work is not in vain: it results in the water staying clear. Likewise, there are times when one must put oneself in order. During such times, one can do nothing for others. But one's work is still valuable. By enhancing one's powers and abilities, through inner development, one will be able to accomplish all the more later on.

5. *A clear, cold spring. One should drink.*

A well fed by a spring of living water is a good well. A man with the virtues of a good well is born to be a leader and saviour of men for he has the water of life. But good fortune is not automatic. Even the best water is useless if it is not brought up. One should drink of the spring of his words and translate them into life.

6. *One draws from the well. No hindrance.*
   It is dependable. Great blessing for all.

The well is for all. No one is forbidden to draw from it. No matter how many come, all find what they need. Likewise, a great man's inner wealth is inexhaustible: the more that people draw from him, the greater does his wealth become. He brings blessing for all.

49

REVOLUTION (FUNDAMENTAL CHANGE)

☰	above	THE JOYOUS, LAKE
☲	below	THE CLINGING, FIRE

THE CONDITION
The image is of fire within the lake.

In OPPOSITION (38), fire above the lake represents opposing tendencies. Here, fire and water combat each other directly, hence the idea of REVOLUTION.

In the four seasons we see REVOLUTION as times and seasons change and, with them, their demands. So also, in the life of peoples and nations, changes call for social reforms.

THE JUDGMENT
Joyousness comes through enlightenment.
If revolution is right, remorse will pass.
On your own day, you are believed.
Persevere, for thereby comes success.

Political revolutions are extremely grave matters to be undertaken only under stress of direst necessity when there is no other way.

Only he with the trust and confidence of the people is called to this task, and then, only when the time is ripe.

But he must proceed in the right way. Just as revolutions in nature, the seasons, accord with fixed laws, so also, political revolutions must follow definite rules:
* One must be able to await the right moment with patience of spirit.
* One must proceed in the right way so that one gladdens the people and, by enlightening them, prevents excesses.
* One must be correct and entirely free of selfish motives.
* The change must answer a real need.

Only then will one have no regrets.

The object of a revolution must be the attainment of clarified, secure conditions to ensure general stability on the basis of what is possible at the moment.

THE IMAGE
As the seasons bring their revolutions,
So the wise man makes clear their times,
And prepares himself for their demands.

In the course of the year, combat between the forces of light and the forces of dark gives rise to the revolution of the seasons. Man masters these changes in nature by noting their regularity, thus bringing order and clarity into apparently chaotic change.

A wise man is able to adjust himself in advance to the demands of changing times.

DEGREES OF CHANGE

1. *Premature revolution: evil results.*
   The time for action has not yet come;
   Be firm in utmost self-restraint.

Changes ought to be undertaken only when there is nothing else to be done. One must be firm in one's own mind, have complete control of oneself and do nothing premature.

2. *Revolution only when one's day comes;*
   Begin now with inner preparation.
   To go to meet it, thus, is no mistake.

Revolution becomes necessary only when all else has failed. Such upheaval must be carefully prepared. There must be available one who has the necessary qualities and who possesses public confidence. But, first, we must consider our inner attitude towards the new condition that will inevitably come. We must, as it were, go to meet it.

3. *Haste or hesitation: both bring danger.*
   When talk has gone around three times,
   Then, may one commit oneself.

When change is necessary, two mistakes must be avoided. Excessive haste and ruthlessness bring disaster. But excessive hesitation and conservatism are also dangerous. Not every call for change should be heeded. But nor, equally, should repeated and well-founded complaints fail of a hearing.

4. *Revolution founded on higher truth*
   Gains support, of itself. Remorse passes.

Radical changes require adequate authority. One must have inner strength as well as influential position. One's actions must correspond with higher truth and must not spring from arbitrary or petty motives. In the end, men will support only that which they feel, instinctively, to be just.

5. *The great man makes the guidelines clear.*
   Thus does he win spontaneous support.

A great man makes things understandable to everyone. Such a man is believed. Through him large, clear guiding lines become visible.

6. *After revolution come the minor reforms.*
   But be satisfied with the attainable.

After large fundamental problems are settled detailed reforms become necessary. Even small people change, at least superficially, to conform to the new order, but it does not go very deep. But if we were to go too far and try to achieve too much it would lead to unrest and misfortune. One's objectives must be limited to what is currently possible.

50
THE GREAT BOWL (SACRED VESSEL)

≡≡ above THE CLINGING, FIRE

≡≡ below THE GENTLE, WOOD, WIND

THE CONDITION
The image of fire, kindled by wood and wind, suggests the preparing of food, nourishment.

In ancient China the ceremonial vessel used to hold food for sacred rites and banquets, and also for family meals, took the form of a great bowl of bronze with legs and ears (its handles) and carrying rings.

It was from such a vessel that the head of the house would serve his honoured guests.

THE WELL (48) also conveys the idea of nourishment; nourishment for all. But here the idea relates to a refined civilisation and to the fostering and nourishment of able and worthy men, to the benefit of all.

THE GREAT BOWL has always been connected with the very heights of Chinese culture.

THE JUDGMENT
THE GREAT BOWL: supreme good fortune.
Herein is the culmination of culture;
Enlightenment and true understanding:
Clarity comes through inner gentleness.

THE WELL likens the nourishment of all to water nourishing growing wood. Here, in turn, wood nourishes flame: the spirit of life.

All that is visible must grow beyond itself, extend into the realm of the invisible, if it is to find firm roots in the cosmic order, in true consecration.

Here is the culmination of civilisation in religion. The Great Bowl serves to offer the highest earthly values to God. But the truly divine is made manifest only in man: in the supreme revelation of God in prophets and holy men. To venerate and honour them is truly veneration of God.

The will of God, as revealed through them, should be accepted in humility, for thereby comes enlightenment and true understanding of the world, thence blessing and success.

THE IMAGE
As fire depends on the wood within it;
As wood within fire lends power to flame;
Thus does a wise man give light to his life.

A wise man succeeds in assigning the right place to life and to fate. He puts them in harmony. In this way does he secure his fate. He keeps his life alight by ensuring that the sources of life are perpetually renewed.

Perpetual renewal gives duration to order.

DEGREES OF CHANGE

1. *A Great Bowl, upturned for cleaning.*
   The lowly are honoured for their works.
In a highly developed civilisation, every person of goodwill can, in some way, succeed. However lowly one may be, the way to gain acceptance is through self-purification. Thus can one attain a station in which one can prove oneself and be recognised.

2. *There is good food in one's Great Bowl.*
   But one is envied. Be cautious. No harm.
In an advanced culture, it is important to strive to achieve something significant. But one's concentration on real work may well cause envy and ill-will in others. Fear not. The more one limits oneself to one's actual achievements, the less harm can the envious inflict. To stay free of entanglements is one's strongest shield.

3. *The handle is bent: one's pheasant wasted.*
   One is impeded, but remorse will pass.
If a bowl's handle is defective it cannot be lifted and used. Until it is repaired, even the richest food cannot be eaten by anyone. If one has good qualities and gifts of mind, yet one is not recognised, it blocks one's effectiveness and one's gifts go to waste. If only one could see: such gifts are truly spiritual: the tension will go in due time.

4. *The legs of the Great Bowl are broken.*
   The prince's meal is spilled
   And his person soiled. Misfortune.
A prince has a difficult and responsible task. If he is not adequate and goes about with inferior people, his work will fail and bring him disgrace. Character and rank are disastrously split. Weak character with honoured rank; meagre knowledge with large plans; little power with heavy responsibility: all these seldom escape disaster.

5. *The Great Bowl has ears of yellow gold.*
Yellow is the colour of the middle way. Hollowness signifies receptivity. A prince will find strong and able helpers if he is approachable, modest, and seeks wise counsel. His receptivity is the handle of his success. He must hold to it.

6. *The Great Bowl has carrying rings of jade.*
Jade is both firm and yet of soft lustre. Here a sage counsels a receptive prince. He is mild and pure as precious jade. When prince and sage complement each other, great blessings are bestowed on all.

51

THE AROUSING (SHOCK)

≡≡ above   THE AROUSING, THUNDER
≡≡ below   THE AROUSING, THUNDER

THE CONDITION

THE AROUSING represents forceful upward movement: a movement so violent that it arouses terror, as does the shock of thunder which arouses fear and trembling.

In spring, thunder stirs from its winter rest within the earth. So too, THE AROUSING also means beginning anew, life reawakening.

In human terms, it represents one who seizes power with energy and force.

THE JUDGMENT

Thunder comes, spreading terror afar;
But shock also brings success and joy,
For now is the time for reverence
As God comes forth in THE AROUSING.

The shock that comes from the manifestation of God makes man afraid. But this fear of God is good, for it leads to joy.

Fear aroused makes one cautious: caution brings measure: measure brings good fortune.

When a man has learned within his heart what fear and trembling mean, then is he safeguarded from terror from without. Thunder may roll and spread terror afar, yet he remains composed, reverent in spirit.

Such is the spirit that must animate leaders and rulers of men: a profound inner seriousness from which all outer terrors glance off harmlessly.

Such is the spirit that must animate the lord of the sacred rites: that he does not let slip the sacred vessel; that he does not allow the sacred moment to be interrupted.

As thunder reverberates afar, so also, a mighty ruler knows how to shape himself to arouse the respect of all; yet is he careful and exact in the smallest detail.

THE IMAGE

Thunder repeated: the image of shock.
Thus, in fear and trembling,
The wise man examines himself
To set his life in order and to shape it.

The shock of continuing thunder brings fear and trembling to all.

The wise man is always filled with reverence at the manifestation of God. He sets his life in order and searches his heart lest it harbour any secret opposition to the will of God. Thus is reverence the foundation of true culture.

DEGREES OF CHANGE

1. *Shock comes, but it leads to laughter.*
   Fear brings good fortune in due course.

When fear and trembling, caused by shock, first come upon one, one sees oneself at a disadvantage as against others. This is only transitory. When the ordeal is over one will experience relief. Thus, the terror one had to endure at the outset brings one good fortune in the long run.

2. *Shock brings danger and great losses,*
   But do not go in pursuit. Withdraw.

When shock endangers one, and one suffers great loss, one should not resist. One should retreat inwardly to heights inaccessible to the forces of outer danger. Accept the loss. When the time of shock and upheaval has passed, one will get one's possessions back. Is not one's self one's greatest good?

3. *Shock that makes one crazed with grief.*
   Be spurred to inner action. No harm.

At times when one suffers the external shock of fate, one's presence of mind is easily lost. One must not mutely let fate take its course; nor overlook the opportunity for action. Let the shock of fate induce movement within so that one may overcome such blows. Become equal to the shock.

4. *Inner movement is mired and tough*
   Because things are not clear enough.

Movement within the mind depends for its success, partly, on circumstances. When there is no resistance to fight, nor a victory to be won, inner movement becomes mired, unclear and crippled. One becomes inert.

5. *Shock upon shock threaten danger;*
   But nothing is lost if one is correct.

Repeated shocks, with no breathing space between them, threaten danger. One should conserve one's strength. Behave correctly. Only thus is one spared the fate of being helplessly tossed hither and thither.

6. *When shock brings ruin and terror,*
   And one is not equal to it, keep still.

Inner shock at its height does rob one of reflection and clarity of vision. When it is impossible to act with presence of mind, the right thing to do is to keep still until composure and clarity are restored. Take warning from your neighbour's excited state. Do not allow yourself to be infected by the agitation. Ignore any gossip. Keep calm. Withdraw in time. Be independent.

52

KEEPING STILL

above   KEEPING STILL, MOUNTAIN

below   KEEPING STILL, MOUNTAIN

THE CONDITION

The trigram, KEEPING STILL, here doubled, has the image of a mountain. It is at rest because the Yang principle, which strives upward by nature, is at the top whilst the Yin principle, whose nature is to move downward, is below. It is the rest of movement that has reached its natural end.

Rest is not an ebbing away of all movement as in the Buddhist concept of Nirvana.

The *I Ching* presents rest as no more (but no less) than a state of polarity that always posits movement as its complement.

In human terms, the hexagram turns upon the difficulty of achieving a quiet heart.

THE JUDGMENT

> *Keeping one's back still*
> *So that restlessness dissolves;*
> *Then, beyond the tumult,*
> *One can perceive the great laws.*

True quiet means keeping still when the time has come to keep still and going forward when the time has come to go forward.

Thus are rest and movement in harmony with the demands of the time. Rest is the end and the beginning of all movement.

To keep one's back still is to keep the self still. In one's back are all the nerve fibres mediating movement. When these are stilled the restless ego dissolves and one is no longer aware of one's personality.

When one has thus become calm, then can one turn to the outside world. No longer does one see in it the struggle and tumult of individual beings. One has that true peace of mind necessary for understanding the great laws of the universe and for acting in harmony with them. He who acts from these deep levels makes no mistakes.

When movement and rest accord with the time their course becomes bright and clear.

THE IMAGE

> *As a mountain keeps still within itself,*
> *Thus a wise man does not permit his will*
> *To stray beyond his situation.*

Though the heart thinks constantly, the movements of the heart, one's thoughts, should restrict themselves within the limits of one's position. Thinking that goes beyond this only makes the heart sore.

104

DEGREES OF CHANGE

1. *To halt, even before beginning to move,*
   Is no mistake. Be patient. Persevere.

The beginning is a time of few mistakes. One is still in harmony with primal innocence and not yet influenced by obscuring interests and desires. Intuitively, one sees things as they really are. If one halts at the beginning, and one has not yet lost the truth, one can find the right way. But only by persistent firmness can one avoid irresolute drifting. One must persevere in keeping still.

2. *One halts in time: but in sorrow,*
   Because one cannot save one's master.

When one serves another, stronger than oneself, one is swept along. But one can still halt on the path of wrongdoing even though one lacks the power to check the other's movement. If he presses forward and will not listen, then, no matter how good one's intentions, one cannot save him.

3. *Making one's back rigid is dangerous.*

Enforced quiet, subduing the self by force, is wrong. A fire, when smothered, changes to acrid smoke. Likewise, to induce calmness by artificial rigidity suffocates the heart and one's meditation is soured. One should not try to force results. Calmness comes naturally from inner composure.

4. *To restrain oneself at the right time*
   Is no mistake. It leads towards peace.

The highest stage of rest, forgetting the ego, has not yet been reached. One is not yet free of the ego's dominance and from the dangers of doubt and unrest. Nevertheless, keeping the heart still is no mistake, as it leads, in time, to the higher level.

5. *By keeping the mouth still*
   One's words have order: remorse passes.

If one is in a dangerous situation, especially if one is not adequate to it, one is inclined to be very free with talk and presumptuous jokes. Injudicious speech invariably gives cause for remorse. Be reserved in speech: let it take ever more definite form: let every occasion for regret vanish.

6. *Peaceful stillness: a great blessing.*

Complete tranquillity is the ultimate end of one's effort. One is at rest, not merely in a small, circumscribed way, in matters of detail, but one has a general resignation to life as a whole and this confers peace in relation to every individual matter.

53
DEVELOPMENT (GRADUAL PROGRESS)

≡≡ **above** THE GENTLE, WOOD, WIND

≡≡ **below** KEEPING STILL, MOUNTAIN

THE CONDITION

A tree that grows on a mountain develops slowly, according to the law of its being.

It does not shoot up like a swamp plant but proceeds gradually. Consequently, it stands firmly rooted.

In human terms, the trigrams' attributes show the way of gradual development:

* stillness and tranquillity within guard against precipitate actions;

* penetration and duration without make development and progress possible.

THE JUDGMENT

DEVELOPMENT means going step by step:
Things must follow their proper course.
Gentleness is adaptable, yet penetrating,
For it proceeds from inner calm.

Gradual development is the correct way for relationships involving cooperation.

The many formalities to be observed in preparing for a marriage, or in the appointment of a minister, should proceed slowly: hasty action would not be wise.

Gradual development must also govern any effort to exert influence on others. The essential factor is self-development: the correct and careful cultivation of one's own personality. No influence exerted by agitators has a lasting effect.

Within the self, also, development must follow the same course, if lasting results are to be achieved. One must cultivate inner calm, for gentleness is the outer form that proceeds from inner calm. When inner calm is combined with adaptability to circumstances it is the inexhaustible source of progress.

But the very gradualness of development makes perseverance essential. It is perseverance alone that prevents slow progress from dwindling to nothing.

THE IMAGE

A mountain tree can be seen from afar:
Thus a wise man abides, in dignity and virtue,
In order to improve the moral order.

Like a tree on a mountain, visible from afar, a wise man abides as an example to those around him. Influence and weight can come only through constant and careful work on one's own moral development.

Influencing others is a slow process.

DEGREES OF CHANGE

1. *A lonely beginning is full of danger.*
When a young man is just starting to make his way in life, he is often lonely and without help. He is surrounded by dangers, so his first steps are slow and hesitant. Naturally, he is much criticised by others. Nevertheless, it is these very difficulties that keep him from being too hasty and so actually help him to make progress in the correct way.

2. *Finding security brings reassurance*
   And eating and drinking in concord.
One's development goes a step further when initial insecurity is overcome and a safe position found in life. This first success gives one confidence to face the future. But be ready to share good luck with others. Consider the wild goose: on finding food, it calls its comrades to come and share it.

3. *One goes too far. One loses one's way.*
If we do not let things develop quietly but, of our own choice, plunge too rashly into a struggle, then it will have bad results. One jeopardises one's own life and also one's family by transgressing the law of natural development. Do not provoke conflict but confine yourself to maintaining your own position and to warding off unfair attacks.

4. *Finding a refuge amid dangers. No blame.*
Life, in its course of development, often brings one to inappropriate situations in which it is difficult to hold one's own without danger. Be sensible and yielding. This is the best way to find a safe place where life can go on, despite being surrounded by dangers. This resting place is temporary.

5. *One is misunderstood and misjudged;*
   But it leads in the end to success.
As life's development approaches its peak, one can easily become isolated and may well be misjudged by the very person upon whom one is dependent: the wife by her husband or the official by his superior. This is the work of dark influences that have wormed their way in. Progress is stopped but, in time, the misunderstanding will be cleared away: reconciliation will come.

6. *Wild geese fly high in perfect order.*
At life's end, one's work stands completed. Wild geese approach heaven by keeping themselves in order: something to look up to. Likewise, the life of one who has attained perfection is a bright light for others.

54

THE MARRYING MAIDEN (LOVE)

above THE AROUSING, THUNDER
below THE JOYOUS, LAKE

THE CONDITION

The hexagram pictures a joyous girl who gladly follows the man of her choice and enters into his house and his family.

In human terms it is concerned with the nature of voluntary relationships.

But the hexagram also has, as it were, a cosmic meaning. The trigrams are traditionally associated with east and west, spring and autumn, the beginning and the end of life. They embrace the whole cycle of life.

THE JUDGMENT

THE MARRYING MAIDEN: joyous in movement.
Love is the basis of all true union:
In heaven and earth, in the cycle of life,
In the tactful reserve of a loving wife.

When a girl enters her husband's family, she should do so with special care. She must not take it upon herself to supplant the established family relationships, for that would bring disorder and tension.

All voluntary human relationships must be conducted with caution and reserve if misfortune is not to befall them.

Whilst legally regulated relationships prescribe a fixed connection between duties and right, relationships based on personal inclination depend entirely, in the long run, on tactful reserve.

As the whole of nature depends on the union of heaven and earth, so also, amongst human beings, true union depends on love.

Love, as the essential principle of relatedness, is the most important factor in all the world's relationships.

In THE MARRYING MAIDEN is described the great meaning of heaven and earth.

THE IMAGE

As thunder stirs the surface of a lake,
So a wise man sees transitory movement
In the light of the eternity of the end.

Every relationship between individuals has, within it, the danger of wrong turnings, misunderstandings and disagreements. One should be constantly mindful of the end.

If we permit ourselves to drift along, we unite and part as a matter of chance. But to fix one's mind on ends that endure is the way to avoid the pitfalls that confront the closer relationships of people.

DEGREES OF CHANGE

1. *The marrying maiden: modest and tactful:*
   She knows how to conduct herself.

A girl marrying into a great family will not rank outwardly as the equal of those within it. If she understands how to fit herself into the pattern of things, her position will be entirely satisfactory and she will feel sheltered in the love of her husband. Similarly, a man may enjoy the personal friendship of a prince and be taken into his confidence. Outwardly, this man must keep tactfully in the background. Although he may feel hampered by this status he must know how to conduct himself. He accomplishes things through his kindliness.

2. *The girl is disappointed and lonely:*
   But a one-eyed man can still see.

Man and wife should work together like a pair of eyes. If a girl is disappointed and lonely because the man of her choice has died or gone away she should not lose the inner light of loyalty.

Likewise, if a man is let down, he should still remain faithful to his duty.

3. *A girl just throws herself away*
   If she seeks to marry at any cost.

Anyone who longs so much for joys that he enters into a position not compatible with self-esteem just throws himself away.

4. *A good girl holds back from marriage;*
   Then marries the right man in due course.

A virtuous girl will not throw herself away, even if she allows the customary time for marriage to slip by. She waits for something before going. In marriage to the man truly intended for her is she rewarded for her purity. Virtue brings its own reward.

5. *The king gave his daughter in marriage,*
   But her gown was not as gorgeous
   As that of the serving-maid.

If a girl of aristocratic birth marries a man of modest means, she must know how to adapt herself to the new situation. She must be free of all vanity of outer adornments. She must forget her rank and devote herself entirely to her husband.

6. *She offers a basket of tainted fruit.*
   Empty form is empty indeed.

If a ritual offering is only superficially fulfilled, solely to respect outward form, then such impiety, such irreverence, bodes no good for the marriage:

55
ABUNDANCE (FULLNESS)

≡≡ above THE AROUSING, THUNDER
     below THE CLINGING, FIRE

THE CONDITION
Thunder and lightning together show forth great power. A climax is indicated.

The hexagram represents a time when the attributes, clarity and action together, bring about greatness and prosperity.

Clarity in movement brings abundance.

THE JUDGMENT
The time of abundance is usually brief,
But be not sad or sorrowing;
Be like the sun at noon,
Illuminating and gladdening all creation.

The hexagram pictures a period of great culture and advanced civilisation. But there are hidden dangers. All things wax and wane in the course of time: this is the law of change. When development has reached its peak it must, inevitably, decline.

The sage, therefore, might feel sad in view of the decline that must follow. But such sadness does not befit him. He should be like the sun at midday. He should give light to the whole world.

Times of abundance require a strong leading personality, free of sorrow, that draws unto itself others of like nature. Only a born ruler of men can bring about a time of outstanding greatness and abundance because his will is directed to what is great.

Extraordinary conditions of abundance cannot be maintained permanently. Abundance can only endure if ever more people are brought to share in it; otherwise, it will turn into its opposite, emptiness.

At times of greatness, there is only one means of making firm the foundations of life, namely, spiritual expansion.

THE IMAGE
As thunder and lightning come together:
Inner clarity with outward action;
Thus does the wise judge decide lawsuits.
He ensures strict and precise penalties.

Thunder and lightning also combine in BITING THROUGH (21), but in reverse order.

Whilst there, the laws are laid down, here they are applied and enforced.

Inner clarity is essential to investigate the facts exactly: outward action ensures the carrying out of just punishments.

DEGREES OF CHANGE

1. *To work with one's destined ruler*
   Is no mistake. But only for so long.

To bring about a time of abundance a union of clarity (wisdom) and energetic action is needed. Two kindred spirits, possessed of these attributes, complement each other and so should work together for a time. Therefore, go forth and make your influence felt. But be warned. To overstep the time limit, to cling to him after the completion of the task, is harmful. One must be able to stop at the right moment.

2. *One sees the major stars at noon:*
   An eclipse looms. Mistrust and hate.

When plots and party intrigues come between a ruler, intent on great achievements, and the able man who could bring them about, taking counter-measures only arouses envy and mistrust and prohibits all movement. If one cannot see one's ruler, one should hold inwardly to the power of truth, for its strength is so great that it can, by its invisible influence, arouse that ruler's will.

3. *One sees even small stars at noon:*
   The eclipse is total. Do nothing. Wait.

The prince is now so eclipsed that even small men can push themselves into the foreground. Even the most able man can do nothing. One is hindered yet one is not at fault. Refrain from action: remain blameless.

4. *One sees the lodestar at noon:*
   The eclipse passes. One meets his prince.

As the eclipse passes, darkness decreases and light returns. Wisdom and energy can now unite and complement each other. (In the first DEGREE energy complements wisdom; here, wisdom complements energy.)

5. *As blessing and fame draw near for one,*
   So does good fortune and blessing for all.

When a ruler is modest and therefore open to counsel, he becomes surrounded by able men who can suggest good lines of action. In this way comes blessing, fame and favour for all.

6. *In his house of abundance he screens himself off.*
   He peers out through the gate but no longer sees anyone.

When a man is arrogant and obstinate he attains the opposite of what he strives for. He seeks abundance and splendour and, at all odds, to be master of his house. But he alienates even his own family. He is hopelessly isolated by his own action.

56
THE WANDERER (THE SEEKER)

above THE CLINGING, FIRE

below KEEPING STILL, MOUNTAIN

THE CONDITION

When grass on a mountain takes fire, it does not linger or tarry in one place but travels on, seeking new fuel.

A wanderer is one who seeks. Strange lands and separation are the wanderer's lot.

Like true greatness, a wanderer has no fixed abode. He has few friends. He cannot easily find his proper place.

The trigrams mean keeping still and adhering to clarity; inwardly steadfast yet yielding; reserved and yet light-giving.

THE JUDGMENT

THE WANDERER: success through smallness.
Perseverance brings him blessing.
The meaning within is truly great.

When a man is a wanderer he should not be gruff or overbearing or give himself airs. He must be cautious and reserved, for in this way he protects himself from evil. If he is obliging towards others, he wins success.

A wanderer has no fixed abode. His home is the road. Let him therefore take care to remain upright and steadfast: that he sojourn only in the proper places, with good people. Thus does he find blessing to go his way unmolested, not provoking ill.

A wanderer who is reserved and unpretentious cannot be humiliated, even though he is in a strange land.

It is a great thing to grasp the inner meaning of THE WANDERER.

THE IMAGE

As fire on a mountain tarries not;
A bright light without, yet calm within;
So the wise judge protracts no lawsuits.
In his judgments, he is clear-minded;
In imposing penalties, he is cautious.

Fire upon a mountain does not linger: it passes on: it is of short duration.

Penalties and lawsuits should be like this. They should be quickly passing matters and not dragged out indefinitely.

Prisons ought to be places where people are lodged only temporarily, as are guests. They must not become dwelling places.

BITING THROUGH (21) and ABUNDANCE (55) are also concerned with lawsuits: they both combine clarity with action. But here is set forth the need for clarity with caution.

DEGREES OF CHANGE

1. *To busy oneself with trivial things*
   Is to mis-spend one's will. Misfortune.

He who consumes his will-power on trifles has no breadth of vision. A wanderer must not demean himself nor busy himself with the inferior or trivial things he meets along the way. The humbler and more defenceless he is outwardly, the more he must preserve his inner dignity. If a stranger hopes to find friends by lending himself to jokes and buffoonery, he will find contempt.

2. *One comes to an inn with one's goods.*
   One wins a servant's steadfastness.

If a wanderer is modest and reserved, he does not lose touch with his inner being (his goods) and so can find rest within. Even so, his outward love for others is not diminished. People like him and further him. Thus does he acquire substance. Moreover, he wins a thing of inestimable value to a wanderer, and that is the steadfastness of a faithful servant.

3. *One's inn burns down. Danger. Unrest.*
   One loses a servant's steadfastness.

A truculent stranger does not know how to behave properly. He meddles in affairs and controversies that do not concern him and so he loses his resting place (the inn within). He treats his servant with aloofness and arrogance and so loses his loyalty. When a stranger in a strange land has no one on whom he can rely, he is really in danger.

4. *One finds a shelter, with one's goods:*
   But be on guard: one is not yet secure.

He who knows how to limit his outward desires and is inwardly strong and aspiring can find, at least, a place of shelter he can stay within. He has acquired inner worth (his goods), but, even with this, he is not secure. He must be always on guard, ready to defend it. Ill at ease, he is still conscious of being a stranger.

5. *He offers his gift. He gains recognition.*
   Even a stranger can find friends.

One wishes to serve a prince, so one offers one's gifts and finds acceptance. One can find a home, even in a strange land, if one knows how to meet the situation.

6. *One lets oneself go. Joy turns to tears.*

Misfortune will overtake the heedless and imprudent. To let oneself go, laughing and jesting, is to forget that one is still a stranger. Joy will turn to weeping. To lose one's modesty is to invite misfortune.

57

THE GENTLE (THE PENETRATING)

≡≡ above   THE GENTLE, WIND, WOOD
≡≡ below   THE GENTLE, WIND, WOOD

THE CONDITION

The image of THE GENTLE is the wind or wood. It means gentleness and adaptability but also penetration. It penetrates everywhere on earth, as does the wind, and into dark places, as do roots within the earth.

In nature, it is the wind that disperses dark clouds to leave the sky clear, serene.

In human life, it is penetrating clarity of judgment that thwarts dark motives.

Such is the powerful influence of a great personality: it uncovers and breaks up dark intrigues that shun the light of day.

THE JUDGMENT

THE GENTLE succeeds through being small.
It furthers one to have a goal in life;
It furthers one to see the great man.

Gentleness succeeds through having a clearly defined goal. It achieves its purpose by ceaseless influence, acting always in the same direction: adaptable yet consistent.

Penetration produces its effects not by violence but gradually and inconspicuously, by influence that never lapses.

Results of this kind are less noticeable than those won by surprise attack but they are more enduring and more complete.

Small strength can achieve its purpose only by subordinating itself to a great man capable of creating order.

Gentleness shows depth of character. Through gentleness one can weigh things and come to understand their inner nature without being in the forefront oneself. Herein lies the power of influence: that one can take special circumstances into account, and make exceptions, without being inconsistent.

THE IMAGE

As winds follow, one upon another;
So the wise ruler spreads his commands.

The power in the wind depends upon its ceaselessness. Time is its instrument.

Like the wind, a wise ruler's thought penetrates the soul of his people. As the wind scatters dark clouds, so he scatters hidden evils. His is a lasting influence that enlightens and instructs so that action is in accord with his will.

Action without prior enlightenment only repels and raises fears.

DEGREES OF CHANGE

1. *Irresolute drifting. No discipline.*
Innate gentleness often leads to indecisiveness. Beset by doubts, one drifts to and fro: too weak either to advance or to retreat resolutely. Consider the warrior. He does resolutely what order demands. Do likewise. If the will wavers, persevere. One can be sustained by discipline. Resolute discipline is better, by far, than irresolute licence.

2. *Penetration into darkest recesses:*
   A great effort of will finds favour.
At times, one has to deal with hidden evils: intangible influences that slink in dark corners and affect people by suggestion. One must trace these back to the most secret recesses in order to deal with them. The effort required is enormous, but worth while, for, only when such elusive influences are brought into the light of day and branded, do they lose their power over people.

3. *Irresolute vacillation. Exhaustion.*
Penetrating reflection must not be pushed too far, lest it exhaust one's will and cripple the power of decision. After a matter has been thoroughly pondered, it is essential to form a decision and to act. Repeated deliberation only brings fresh doubts and scruples. It leads to humiliation because one shows oneself to be unable to act.

4. *A man of merit: both modest and energetic.*
To combine innate modesty with energetic action is a great virtue. In one of rank and experience, possession of such virtue is an assurance of success. Such a man reveres God and honours the worthy, yet he does not overlook the everyday needs of man.

5. *Steadfast, careful work. Good fortune.*
Even bad beginnings can turn out well if one is steadfast, firm and correct. When reforms are called for, steadfastness is crucial. Before the change, ponder again and again. After the change, note the effects with care, to see if the improvements are real. To make right a bad start, one must be impartial.

6. *Penetrating the dark, one loses oneself.*
The penetrating mind can follow injurious influences into the most secret corners. But it is definitely harmful to persist in attempting to penetrate the domain of darkness if, thereby, one no longer has the strength to combat such things decisively. He who goes this way will lose his self.

58
THE JOYOUS

☱☱ above THE JOYOUS, LAKE
below THE JOYOUS, LAKE

THE CONDITION
THE JOYOUS is symbolised by the smiling lake which refreshes and rejoices all life.

True joy rests on firmness and strength within, manifesting itself outwardly as yielding and gentle.

THE JUDGMENT
THE JOYOUS succeeds through steadfastness;
For, if one is both joyous and steadfast,
One accords with both God and man.

The joyous mood is infectious and so can achieve something among men. But joy must be based on steadfastness if it is not to degenerate into uncontrolled mirth.

Truth and strength must dwell within the heart, whilst gentleness reveals itself in social intercourse. In this way one assumes the right attitude towards both God and man and, so, can achieve something.

Under certain conditions, the intimidation of others, without gentleness, may achieve something momentarily: but not for all time.

When men's hearts are won by friendship, they will forget their drudgery; they will willingly take hardships upon themselves; they will, if need be, not shun even death itself; so great is the power of joy over men.

The greatest thing in making the people joyous is that they encourage one another. Herein is found the best way of government: to lead the people joyously.

To be inwardly firm and outwardly gentle is the way of true joy.

THE IMAGE
As two lakes join to replenish each other,
So the wise man joins with his friends
To discuss and practise the truths of life.

Two lakes joined together will not dry up so readily, for each replenishes the other.

Likewise, knowledge should be a refreshing and vitalising force. It becomes so, only through stimulating intercourse with congenial friends, with whom one can hold discussion and practise the application of the truths of life.

In this way, learning becomes many-sided and takes on a cheerful lightness; whereas there is always something ponderous and one-sided about the learning of the self-taught.

116

DEGREES OF CHANGE

1. *Contented joyousness: inner security;*
   One's way is not yet hedged by doubt.

Firmness and modesty are the prerequisites of harmonious joy. The doubts and scruples that interfere with joy are still far away. Here is a quiet, wordless, self-contained joy that desires nothing from without and rests content with everything. It remains free of selfish likes and dislikes. Such freedom is blessed because it harbours the quiet security of a heart fortified within itself.

2. *Sincere joyousness dispels remorse,*
   If one has faith in one's will.

One is often in the company of inferior people, in whose company one is tempted by pleasures inappropriate for the superior man. To participate in such low pleasures will bring remorse. It is by trusting oneself, by not permitting one's will to swerve, by one's sincerity towards others, that one finds respect. Then, even dubious companions will not venture to proffer base pleasures.

3. *When joy comes from without: misfortune:*
   For it causes one to lose oneself.

True joy springs from within. He who is empty within welcomes idle pleasures as diversions. He lacks inner stability and so needs to be amused. He will always find opportunity for indulgence. He attracts external pleasures by the emptiness of his nature. As they overwhelm him, he loses himself more and more.

4. *In weighing joys, one is not at peace:*
   But in choosing the higher is true joy.

In weighing the choice between different kinds of pleasure, the higher or the lower, one has no inner peace. Passion leads to suffering. So turn away from the lower and strive for the higher. Seal the decision, fix the will, for this is the way to true joy and peace.

5. *Disintegrating influences. Beware.*

Dangerous elements approach even the best of men. One must have nothing to do with them for their disintegrating influence will act slowly but surely. Recognise the danger for then can one protect oneself from harm.

6. *Seductive joyousness: he loses himself.*

A vain nature invites diverting pleasures and suffers accordingly. Base pleasures can seduce and gain such a hold over a man that he is swept along by them. He has already given up the direction of his own life. He now depends, utterly, upon chance and external influences.

59
DISPERSION (THE DISSOLVING)

≡≡
≡ ≡ above   THE GENTLE, WIND
≡≡
≡ ≡ below   THE ABYSMAL, WATER

THE CONDITION
When the wind blows over water, it disperses it, dissolving it into foam and mist.

In GATHERING TOGETHER (45) elements that have been parted unite as do waters in a lake. DISPERSION shows the way to reunion by the dissolving of divisive egotism.

As wind penetrates the surface of water to disperse it, so also, by penetrating the consciousness of men, is disunity overcome and divisive rigidity dissolved.

When a man's vital energy is dammed up within him (danger within), it is gentleness that serves to dissolve the blockage.

THE JUDGMENT
DISPERSION shows the way to reunion.
The temple is the place of union.
Union is the time for great undertakings.

Religious forces are needed to overcome the egotism that divides men. The common celebration of great feasts and sacred rites expresses and articulates the social unity of family and of state. Splendour and sacred music serve to arouse strong tides of emotion for all hearts to share in unison.

Thus is awakened consciousness of the One Creator: the common origin of all life.

Thus is awakened the common will: the co-operation among men so necessary for great general undertakings that set a high goal for the will of the people.

Let barriers dissolve; all hands unite.

But only a man who is himself free of all selfish, ulterior considerations, and who perseveres in steadfastness and justice, can dissolve the hardness of egotism.

THE IMAGE
As the warm winds of spring stir the waters
And dissolve even the rigidity of ice;
So wise kings of old built temples
To praise God; to stir and unite men.

As the warm winds of spring come, they break up the rigidity of ice floes to be reunited within their original nature.

Through hardness and selfishness, hearts grow rigid: rigidity leads to separation from others: egotism isolates. But when men are shaken by religious awe in the face of eternity, when stirred by intuition of the One Creator, they become united as one.

DEGREES OF CHANGE

1. *When divergence emerges, act quickly.*
Disunion should be overcome at the outset, before it has become complete. When hidden divergences in temper make themselves felt and lead to mutual misunderstandings, one should take quick and vigorous action to dissolve the misunderstandings and mutual mistrust. Be like the wind, dispersing the clouds before they can bring a storm.

2. *When one finds oneself alienated,*
   Be objective, moderate and just.
If one finds within oneself the seeds of alienation, hatred and ill-humour, one must quickly set about dissolving these obstructions. Hatred will achieve nothing. Be of goodwill, moderate and just in judgment, for thus is ill-will dissolved and all cause for remorse will disappear. Thus does one regain an unblocked view of humanity.

3. *To dissolve one's self is no mistake.*
If one's work becomes so difficult that one can no longer think of oneself, one should set aside all personal desires, disperse inner barriers and direct the will outwards. To have a goal, a great task, outside oneself is the way to attain self-dissolution without regret. Only by great renunciation can one gain the strength for great achievements.

4. *Dissolving oneself from one's own party*
   Brings supreme good fortune.
In great tasks for the general welfare, all private friendships must be left out of account. Only by rising above party interests can anything truly great be achieved. One must have the courage to forego what is near to win what is afar. Ordinary men do not think of such things. To comprehend, one must have a wider view of life such as only unusual men attain. Dispersion leads to accumulation.

5. *A great idea: a rallying point.*
In times of dispersion and separation, a great idea can provide a focal point for organising recovery: salvation, in a time of deadlock. A ruler who can dispel misunderstandings is a great rallying point.

6. *Dissolving one's self to save oneself.*
   To avoid danger this way is no mistake.
A man may be required to rescue not only himself, but also his kin, by keeping away from an existing danger or finding a way out of a danger already upon them. Here, by going this way, he does what is right.

60

LIMITATION (DUE MEASURE)

☵ above   THE ABYSMAL, WATER
☱ below   THE JOYOUS, LAKE

THE CONDITION

Whilst water is inexhaustible, a lake is something limited: that is its peculiarity: if more water comes into it, it overflows.

The Chinese word for limitation denotes the joints that divide a bamboo stalk.

In day-to-day terms, it means the thrift that sets fixed limits upon expenditures.

In relation to the moral sphere, it means the limits a wise man sets for himself: the limits of loyalty and disinterestedness.

THE JUDGMENT

LIMITATION, due measure, leads to success.
But do not persist in galling restraint,
For its way comes to an end, to failure.

Limitations are tiresome, but valuable.

If we live economically in normal times, we are prepared for times of want. Thus, to be sparing frees one from humiliation.

Limitations are also indispensable in the regulation of world conditions.

In nature, fixed limits for day and night, summer and winter, give time its meaning.

In the same way economy, by setting fixed limits upon expenditures, preserves goods and prevents injury to people.

In the creation of institutions, limits prevent encroachment upon property and serve to regulate spheres of operation.

But, in setting limits, we must observe due measure. He who seeks to impose galling limitations upon his own nature brings injury to himself. And if he were to go too far in imposing limitations on others, they would only rebel. Therefore, it is necessary to set limits even upon limitation.

THE IMAGE

As does a lake limit the inexhaustible;
So does the wise man weigh and measure.
He finds virtue in where his duty lies.

As a lake needs limitations, so too, one achieves significance in life by setting limits, by discrimination. Discriminations are the backbone of morality. Unlimited possibilities are unsuited to man: his life would then dissolve into the boundless. To become strong one needs the limitations, freely accepted, that one's duty ordains. Only thus can one's spirit be made free.

Self-limitation is the basis of freedom.

DEGREES OF CHANGE

1. *One's actions are limited. No blame.*
   Be discreet in limiting one's words.

Often one wants to undertake something but finds oneself confronted by insurmountable limitations. Recognise these limits and know where to stop for, by not going beyond one's limits, one accumulates the energy to enable one, in due time, to act with great force. Discretion is the key to preparing the way for momentous things. Disorder begins with words. Thus is a wise man careful in limiting his words and his actions.

2. *To limit one's action brings misfortune.*

When the time for action has come, the moment must be quickly seized. Hesitation is correct when the time has not yet come, but once the obstacles have been removed, anxious hesitation is a mistake. Water collects, first, in a lake without flowing out. But when it is full it finds an outlet. So it is, in the life of man.

3. *To know no limitation: cause for lament.*
   But if one laments, one finds freedom.

Extravagance leads to regret. A man bent only on pleasures loses his sense of the limits he needs. He must not seek to blame others but realise his mistakes are of his own making. Only thus is he freed from error.

4. *Natural, contented limitation. Success.*

Limitation that requires persistent effort consumes energy. Water is limited, by nature, to flowing downhill. Natural limitations lead to success by saving inner energy. Avoid vain struggles. Save your energy so that it may be wholly applied to benefit the matter in hand. The success of natural, contented limitation lies in adaptability.

5. *Sweet limitation through self-limitation.*
   This is the way to favour and esteem.

Limitation must be carried out correctly, if it is to be effective. To impose limits on others, whilst evading them ourselves, invites resentment, provokes resistance. Limiting oneself first, sweetens it for all.

6. *Galling limitation. To persist is bad.*
   But, even so, one must save oneself.

Consistent severity inevitably leads to reaction. People will not endure excessive restriction. The body will rebel against excessive asceticism. But sometimes, such ruthlessness towards oneself is the only way to expiate guilt and save one's self.

61
INNER TRUTH

≡≡ above THE GENTLE, WIND
≡≡ below THE JOYOUS, LAKE

THE CONDITION
When the wind blows over a lake it stirs the surface by penetrating it. We see the visible effect of an invisible force. Such is the force of INNER TRUTH.

The hexagram, open at the centre, pictures a humble heart, free of all prejudice, and therefore open to the truth.

The attributes, joyousness within and gentleness without, show the basis of great achievements: joy in obeying one's superiors and gentle forbearance towards inferiors.

THE JUDGMENT
INNER TRUTH is a forceful influence:
It penetrates even the unhearing heart.
Its way is through deep understanding.
The force of inner truth must grow great indeed before its influence can extend to those most difficult to influence.

In dealing with intractable persons, the whole secret of success lies in finding the right approach. One must first rid oneself of all prejudice and let the mind of the other person act on one without restraint. Thus can one establish contact with him and understand him. Only when this door has been opened, can the force of one's personality begin to influence him.

If, in this way, one finds no obstacle insurmountable, one can undertake even the most dangerous enterprises and succeed.

But it is important to understand upon what the force of inner truth depends. Its force is not like simple intimacy or common interest: such ties exist among thieves. Common interest holds only for so long: when the community of interest ceases, the holding together also ceases, Only when the bond is based upon what is right, upon steadfastness, will it remain so firm that it triumphs over everything.

THE IMAGE
As wind stirs water by penetration;
Thus does the wise judge understand men.
A wise man, obliged to judge the mistakes of others, tries to penetrate their minds to gain a sympathetic appreciation of the circumstances. A deep understanding that knows how to pardon can make a strong moral impression. Such mildness springs not from weakness but from superior clarity.

DEGREES OF CHANGE

1. *Inner truth comes of inner stability:*
   But secret designs, of inner disquiet.

The force of inner truth depends on inner stability, a preparedness of mind. But to cultivate secret, exclusive bonds deprives one of inner independence. To rely upon the support of others generates disquiet and anxiety within. One departs from the way of inner peace: the force of inner truth is lost.

2. *Inner truth finds the responsive heart.*

A crane may be quite hidden when it makes its call, yet its young will recognise it and respond, even from afar. Likewise, a feeling voiced in truth and frankness exerts a mysterious and far-reaching influence. Kindred spirits, the inwardly receptive, are the first to respond, but the circle then grows larger and larger. The root of all influence lies in one's inner being. But any deliberate striving for effect destroys all possibility of producing it.

Since ones's words and deeds exert such influence, near or far, bringing one honour or shame, must one not, then, be cautious?

3. *He finds a comrade; becomes dependent.*
   Now he sobs; now he sings.

If the source of one's strength lies not in oneself but in one's relation to other people, if one's centre of gravity depends on them, then one is inevitably tossed to and fro between joy and sorrow. One must judge: 'Is this an affliction or the joy of love?'

4. *One turns oneself away to seek the light,*
   As the moon turns to face the sun.

As the moon receives light from the sun, so, to intensify the power of inner truth, one must turn to one's superior, from whom one receives enlightenment. One must be humble and reverent to face the light. But one also needs the will to turn oneself away from one's comrades and towards the superior.

5. *In possessing truth, he holds together.*

A ruler, by the power of his personality, unifies and knits together his adherents. Without such power, in truth, at its centre unity is deceptive and unreliable.

6. *Cockcrowing that persists. Misfortune.*

A cock is dependable. It crows at dawn. But to crow all day would invite misfortune. A man's words may succeed, now and then, in awakening faith, but to persist and exaggerate will have bad consequences.

62

GREAT SMALLNESS

☳ above   THE AROUSING, THUNDER
☶ below   KEEPING STILL, MOUNTAIN

THE CONDITION

The hexagram indicates an exceptional situation: a time of transition.

Exceptional conditions are also indicated in GREAT HEAVINESS (28), where four strong lines are enclosed by two weak lines.

There, the strong element necessarily creates struggle and enforces its will: here, it is the weak element that must mediate with the outside world.

The line pattern suggests a soaring bird. A bird should not try to surpass itself and attempt to fly into the sun. It should descend to earth, to where its nest is.

GREAT HEAVINESS is like a beam: its danger lies in excessive weight.

GREAT SMALLNESS is like a bird: its danger lies in mounting too high and losing the ground under its feet.

If one occupies a position of authority for which one is, by nature, inadequate, extraordinary prudence is necessary.

THE JUDGMENT

> *Going with the time leads to success:*
> *Work on small things, not great things.*
> *The flying bird brings the message:*
> *'Strive not upward; better to stay below'.*

Exceptional modesty and conscientiousness are sure to succeed. But it is important that they do not become empty form, fawning or servile. They must always be combined with correct dignity in personal behaviour, if one is not to throw oneself away.

One must understand the demands of the time in order to offset its difficulties.

One must not, in any event, count on success: the requisite strength is lacking.

One should not strive after lofty things, but hold to lowly things.

THE IMAGE

> *Thunder on the mountain: loud and near.*
> *The wise man derives an imperative.*

The wise man understands the time and learns its message. He must fix his eyes more closely and more directly on duty than does the ordinary man, even at the risk of appearing petty. Such a man is reverent in worship, sensitive, dutiful, unpretentious.

His significance lies in that, in external matters, he is on the side of the lowly.

DEGREES OF CHANGE

1. *The fledgling tries to fly too soon.*
One should put up with the traditional ways as long as possible, otherwise one exhausts oneself and still achieves nothing. If one will not be restrained but seeks to soar like a bird, one wilfully endangers oneself. Extraordinary measures should be resorted to only when all else has failed. If a bird tries to fly up when it is time to keep still then the hunter will surely have it.

2. *Seek not to surpass one's master.*
Extraordinary restraint is no mistake in exceptional times. If one seeks a prince, but meets only an official, one must accept the situation, not try to force anything, and conscientiously go about one's duty.

3. *Danger unseen. Take extreme care:*
   One may be struck from behind.
A strong man, knowing he is in the right, may disdain to hold himself on guard because he considers it petty. He goes his way proud and unconcerned. But his self-confidence deludes him. Dangers lurk for which he is unprepared. One can avoid this if one understands that the time demands special attention to little details.

4. *When tempted to take the initiative,*
   Be on guard, do not act, be steadfast.
One is tempted to move, to force one's way to the goal, to by-pass others. But this leads to danger. One must be very careful and inwardly steadfast to avoid mistakes.

5. *Dense clouds gather, but still no rain.*
   The time of transition is now very near,
   So the prince seeks out the best man.
As transition comes, dense clouds give the promise of rain to relieve the tension. But still it does not come: the clouds achieve nothing. Likewise, in exceptional times, a born ruler may be qualified to set the world in order and shower blessings on all people, but he can achieve nothing if he stands alone and without help. In seeking helpers he must be modest. He must count not fame, but genuine achievements. Thus can he find the right man for great tasks.

6. *The bird that flies higher and higher.*
If one overshoots the goal, presses on, cannot call a halt, one is already arrogant. One draws upon oneself misfortune by going against the time. Like an exhausted bird, one falls, eventually, into the hunter's net.

63

ORDER (AFTER COMPLETION)

☵ above   THE ABYSMAL, WATER
☲ below   THE CLINGING, FIRE

THE CONDITION

This hexagram is the evolution of PEACE (11).

The transition from confusion to order is complete: everything is in its proper place.

The condition is favourable, yet it gives reason for thought, for it is just when perfect equilibrium has been reached that any movement may cause disorder to return.

The natural development of ORDER is towards STANDSTILL (12), stagnation. Hence, the present condition indicates a time of climax that requires the utmost caution.

THE JUDGMENT

ORDER leads to disorder. Be persevering.
A time for success, only in small matters.

The transition from the old time to the new is already accomplished: it is a time of great cultural refinement.

In principle, everything stands in order, systematised, and it is only in details that success can still be achieved.

However, we must not allow ourselves to relax and let things take their course without taking care over details.

Such indifference is the root of all evil: it inevitably leads to decay.

Here we have the rule indicating the usual course of history. But this rule is not an inescapable law. He who understands it is in a position to avoid its effects by dint of unremitting perseverance and caution.

THE IMAGE

Water over fire: a time of perfect order.
But the wise man considers misfortune
And arms himself against it in advance.

The trigrams, water over fire, give the image of a kettle, hanging over a fire, so that the two elements stand in relation. They generate energy (steam) only by the careful relating of elements that do not mix and are, by nature, hostile to each other.

This balance demands utmost care. If the water boils over, the fire will be put out and the energy lost: if the heat is too great, the water will dry up.

In life, too, there are times when all forces are in balance, working in harmony, and all seems to be in the best of order. Then, only the sage recognises the moments that bode danger and knows how to avoid it.

DEGREES OF CHANGE

1. *One stops in time. No blame.*
In times following a great transition, everything is pressing forward, striving for development and progress. But this, at the beginning, is not good. It overshoots moderation and leads to loss and collapse. A strong man does not allow himself to be infected by the general intoxication but checks his course in time. He may not remain entirely untouched by the general pressure, but he suffers no real harm because his behaviour is correct.

2. *When trust is withheld,*
   Turn inward and wait. Develop within.
One in public life wants to achieve something, but is not receiving the confidence of those in authority, which he needs, so to speak, for his personal protection. Especially in times of order, those with power may grow arrogant, conceited, and fail to foster new talent. One must not seek office by throwing oneself away. Be calm. Times change. Wait. Develop inner worth. One need only be able to wait.

3. *An emperor conquers new lands. Danger.*
In a time of order, a ruler's mind may turn to forceful colonial expansion. But if territory won at bitter cost is regarded as a place to employ inferior people, who are thought to be good enough for the colonies, there is no chance of success. In the same way, dangers attend every enterprise ambitious to expand.

4. *Even the finest clothes*
   Will turn, eventually, to rags.
In times of flowering culture, occasional social upheavals uncover hidden evils in society. But it is soon forgotten, glossed over or concealed. But the wise man does not neglect such grave omens. Only thus can one avert the evil consequences.

5. *Simplicity is more blessed*
   Than much display without warmth.
Times of great culture also influence the sacred forms. Old, simple forms are replaced by ever more elaborate ritual and outward display. Inner seriousness is endangered. God looks into the heart.

6. *After crossing a stream, keep going.*
   Turning back is dangerous. Go forward.
There is a fascination in looking back on a peril overcome. But such vain self-admiration brings misfortune. Go forward. Do not look back. Thus can one escape this danger.

64

TRANSITION (BEFORE COMPLETION)

≡≡ above   THE CLINGING, FIRE

≡≡ below   THE ABYSMAL, WATER

THE CONDITION

This hexagram represents a time of change: of transition from disorder (danger) to order (clarity): a change not yet completed.

Nature presents a parallel in springtime: a time of transition from the stagnation of winter to the fruitfulness of summer.

THE JUDGMENT

> *During transition, caution brings success.*
> *A prick-eared old fox can cross the ice,*
> *But the rash young fox gets his tail wet.*

Conditions are most difficult: the task is great and full of responsibility. It is nothing less than leading the world out of confusion and back to order.

But it is a task that promises success because there is a goal that can unite the forces now tending in different directions. At first, however, one must move warily, like an old fox walking over ice.

The caution of a fox walking over ice is proverbial in China. His ears are constantly alert to the cracking of the ice as he carefully and circumspectly searches out the safest spots. But a young fox who has not, as yet, acquired this caution goes ahead boldly, so he falls in and gets his tail wet. Even though he is almost across the water, still will his effort have been all in vain.

Accordingly, in times before completion, during transition, deliberation and caution are the prerequisites of success.

THE IMAGE

> *Fire and water are opposites by nature,*
> *So a wise man differentiates with care.*
> *He separates things in order to unite them,*
> *That each should find its proper place.*

Fire and water have opposite effects. If we wish to accomplish something, achieve a result, then we must first investigate the nature of the forces concerned and ascertain their proper places. If we can bring these forces to bear in the right place, they will have their desired effects and completion will be achieved.

But in order to handle external forces properly, we must, above all, arrive at the correct standpoint ourselves, for only from this vantage can we work correctly.

To try to force completion is harmful.

DEGREES OF CHANGE

1. *One gets one's tail wet. Humiliation.*
In times of disorder there is a temptation to advance oneself as rapidly as possible to get results. But if the time is not yet right, this enthusiasm leads only to failure. One's tail gets wet because one cannot take the end into view: one is too rash. It is better to spare oneself and to hold back.

2. *One holds back. Good. Now be patient.*
The time to act has still not yet come. The patience one needs is not idle waiting but a development of inner strength that will enable one to go forward in due time. Patience, in the highest sense, means putting brakes on strength. One must not fall asleep and lose sight of the goal but remain strong and steadfast in one's resolve.

3. *The time to act has come. Seek helpers.*
   But to force things brings misfortune.
The time of transition has arrived but one lacks the strength to complete the crossing. If one should attempt to force it, disaster would result because collapse would then be unavoidable. What is to be done? A new situation must be created. One must engage the energies of able helpers and then, in fellowship, take the decisive step forward. In this way does completion become possible.

4. *When the struggle comes, be steadfast.*
Now is the time of struggle. To complete the transition we must make ourselves strong in resolution. In such grave times of struggle all misgivings must be silenced. It is a battle, no less, to break and discipline the Devil's forces of decadence. But the struggle also has its reward, for now is the time to lay firm foundations for future mastery.

5. *The light of the wise man is true.*
The victory has been won. Perseverance and steadfastness have been justified and all misgivings overcome. The clarity of the wise man shines forth anew as a rallying point. A new time has arrived. As the beauty of sunshine is redoubled after rain, so the new era appears all the more glorious in contrast with the misery of the old.

6. *Drinking of wine in celebration:*
   But he who wets his head will lose it.
At the dawning of a new age there is trust and conviviality. But keep within proper bounds. He who wets his head (gets drunk) knows no moderation: he spoils his blessing.

TABLE OF HEXAGRAMS

with the Trigrams' Chinese names

TRIGRAMS UPPER ▶ LOWER ▼	Ch'ien ☰	Chên ☳	K'an ☵	Kên ☶	K'un ☷	Sun ☴	Li ☲	Tui ☱
Ch'ien ☰	1	34	5	26	11	9	14	43
Chên ☳	25	51	3	27	24	42	21	17
K'an ☵	6	40	29	4	7	59	64	47
Kên ☶	33	62	39	52	15	53	56	31
K'un ☷	12	16	8	23	2	20	35	45
Sun ☴	44	32	48	18	46	57	50	28
Li ☲	13	55	63	22	36	37	30	49
Tui ☱	10	54	60	41	19	61	38	58

LIST OF TRIGRAMS

	Name	Attributes	Image
☰	THE CREATIVE	strong, active	HEAVEN
☷	THE RECEPTIVE	devoted, yielding	EARTH
☳	THE AROUSING	inciting movement	THUNDER
☵	THE ABYSMAL	dangerous	WATER
☶	KEEPING STILL	resting, calm, firm, quiet	MOUNTAIN
☴	THE GENTLE	penetrating, enduring	WIND, WOOD
☲	THE CLINGING	light-giving, clarity	FIRE
☱	THE JOYOUS	joyousness	LAKE